THE ROUGH GUIDE to

Android™ Phones

by
Andrew Clare

ROUGH
GUIDES

www.roughguides.com

Credits

The Rough Guide to Android Phones	Rough Guides Reference
Text and design: Andrew Clare	Director: Andrew Lockett
Editing: Kate Berens	Editors: Kate Berens, Peter Buckley, Tom Cabot,
Proofreading: Susannah Wight	Tracy Hopkins, Matthew Milton, Joe Staines
Production: Rebecca Short	

Publishing information

This first edition published January 2011 by
Rough Guides Ltd, 80 Strand, London, WC2R 0RL
375 Hudson Street NY 100014, USA
Email: mail@roughguides.com

Distributed by the Penguin Group:
Penguin Books Ltd, 80 Strand, London, WC2R 0RL
Penguin Group (USA), 375 Hudson Street, NY 10014, USA
Penguin Group (Australia), 250 Camberwell Road, Camberwell, Victoria 3124, Australia
Penguin Group (New Zealand), Cnr Rosedale and Airborne Roads, Albany, Auckland, New Zealand
Rough Guides are represented in Canada by Tourmaline Editions Inc., 662 King Street West,
Suite 304, Toronto, Ontario M5V 1M7

Printed and bound by Toppan Security Printing Pte. Ltd.
Typeset in Minion and Myriad
Cover Design: Peter Buckley & Andrew Clare
The Android Robot image on pp. 9, 12, 89 and 111 and on the cover of this book is reproduced from
work created and shared by Google and used according to terms described in the Creative Commons
3.0 Attribution License. Portions of pages 133, 145, 151, 159, 171, 175, 183, 193, 201, 207 and 223 are
modifications based on work created and shared by Google and used according to terms described in the
Creative Commons 3.0 Attribution License.

240 pages; includes index

A catalogue record for this book is available from the British Library.

ISBN 13: 978-1-40538-282-3

3 5 7 9 8 6 4 2

Contents

contents

Introduction

If you've picked up this book, you probably already own an Android™ phone or are thinking about getting one. You'll be in good company: over the last year or so Google™'s mobile platform has become increasingly popular, appearing on more and more phones, made by more and more manufacturers, right across the globe. It's quickly risen up to challenge long established mobile operating systems, thanks to its openness, versatility and speed. You'll find it easy to set up an Android-powered phone exactly the way you like. And with the thousands of apps available from the Android Market™ built to take full advantage of your phone's hardware features, chances are you'll be so overwhelmed with new possibilities and ways to use it that you'll forget that you can actually use it to make calls.

Manufacturers have embraced the freedom offered by Android's open source code to customize how their handsets look and feel, so that exactly what you see onscreen and which button does what comes in a whole spectrum of different flavours.

As Google roll out their own improved user interface elements for the platform, this diverse range of products do seem to be converging toward a common feature set, but currently the task of writing anything resembling a universal manual for Android phones would be as unwieldy as writing a user guide for, say, *The Computer*, encompassing all the different operating systems and hardware options.

Your phone's user manual already does a great job of taking you through the features and functions of your particular handset, and you'll find it an invaluable resource for referring to specifics when perusing the pages of this book. If your phone didn't come with a full printed copy of its manual, you may find it in PDF format on an accompanying CD, or waiting for you on the phone's internal SD storage (see p.107), or on the manufacturer's website.

What this book does is to go beyond the proprietary nuts and bolts stuff in your user manual and help you explore **new ways to use your phone**, showing you some of the **best apps** currently kicking around on the Android Market while helping you sift through the **technical stuff** enough to know what's going on behind that dinky little screen. It will help you get your **email** and **social networks** connected and **synced up** with the minimum of fuss, and dish out all kinds of **tips** from **customizing** your **home screen** to maximizing **battery power**. If you don't own an Android phone yet but are thinking of making the leap, there's also a handy **buying guide** to help you figure out what to look for.

About this book

Text written like **this** denotes a command or label as it appears on either a computer's screen or the phone's screen. Something written like **this** refers to the name of an app that can be downloaded from the Android Market.

This book was written using HTC Desire and Nexus One phones, both running Android 2.2. Although great lengths have been taken to ensure that information in this book is applicable to as many variations of the Android platform as possible, we cannot guarantee that everything mentioned will be accurate for your specific handset.

Acknowledgements

Thanks to Kate Berens, Peter Buckley and Andrew Lockett for their help and guidance while making this book.

Thanks also to Dave Clare and Tom Barnes, and to Anna de Paula Hanika at Google for their answers to my relentless technical queries, and to Iris Balija for her support and encouragement.

primer

What you need to know…

…but were afraid to ask

General questions

What is Android?

Android™ is an open mobile platform developed by Google™. It sits on your phone in much the same way that a computer operating system resides on your Mac or PC, controlling all the hardware functions and providing a solid base for other programs such as web browsers, email clients, media players and so on. You can use it to do many of the same things you can with a computer, plus loads more.

The Android platform is open-source – meaning that Google has made the source code behind the technology openly available to third-party developers – and freely customizable. Companies making handsets designed to run on Android often develop their own UI, or user interface, each with a distinct look and feel and their own slant on

Android comes in many flavours, all of them sweet! But behind the cute branding you'll find a powerful set of features.

what is essentially a common set of core features. So, while the display and icons on your own phone may differ from the images you see in this book, don't let it throw you too much as the basic functions are the same.

As well as managing a phone's hardware and included software, the Android platform can also run applications from third-party developers. Tens of thousands of these "apps" are currently downloadable from the Android Market™ (covered in detail starting on p.111), allowing you to do anything from updating your Facebook status to identifying constellations in the night sky.

As you'd expect from a Google product, Android also integrates tightly with the many Google services you may already subscribe to, such as Gmail™, Google Maps™, Google Docs™, Picasa™, YouTube™ and others.

Android has come along in leaps and bounds since its launch in 2008, with exciting new features and enhancements built into each consecutive release. As well as going by the usual release numbers, these are code named alphabetically after a different kind of dessert. So far we've had Cupcake, Donut, Eclair and Froyo (short for frozen yogurt). To celebrate each new release, Google places a giant sculpture of its namesake on the lawn in front of their California offices.

Current features in 2.2 (Froyo) include:

▶ An integrated camera, camcorder and gallery (see p.42)

▶ Uploading videos and pictures to the web directly from the phone (see p.105)

▶ Text-to-speech and speech-to-text (see p.22)

▶ HTML5 and Adobe Flash support (see p.65)

▶ Google Maps (p.146)

▶ Microsoft Exchange support (see p.92)

▶ Multi-touch support (p.20)

▶ Bluetooth 2.1 (see p.49)

▶ Live Wallpapers and multiple home screens (see p.24)

▶ USB tethering and Wi-Fi hotspot functionality (p.48)

▶ Support for installing applications to an SD memory card (p.127).

Anticipated features for future releases may include an Android Market music store, media streaming from a computer's media library and a revamped user interface.

Sounds impressive, but how does an Android phone compare to other smartphones?

The main contender to Android is the Apple's iOS for the iPhone. There are other phone platforms in circulation – Nokia's Symbian and Microsoft's Windows Mobile have been around on smartphones for some years now. Each has its loyal followers but has been gradually squeezed out of the market by the current crop of iPhone and Android handsets. The iPhone OS currently has the edge on Android when it comes to power management, and integration with Apple services, which, if you're a Mac user or have the bulk of your music collection tied up with iTunes, would probably swing you in that direction. It's also well documented that the iPhone's out-of-the-box virtual keyboard is a little easier to work with than some other touchscreen keyboards, although with Android you have the option of installing an improved one through the Android Market, plus of course some handsets slide open to reveal a physical keyboard and touchpad.

Where the Android platform really shines, though, is with features such as its multitasking abilities – the ability to run several applications in the background (although Apple's iOS4 now also provides a degree of this functionality). Android also supports Adobe's Flash technology which is used to provide video or animation on millions of sites, and works seamlessly with Google services like Google Maps and Gmail.

In comparison to iOS, Android's look and feel is less proprietary. You'll have more control over your phone's appearance and behaviour, and be able to manage your files and data simply and effectively from your computer without having to mediate this process through a program like iTunes.

What's more, Android apps can request direct access to a phone's notification system (like, for example, the beep you get when you receive an SMS text message), so you can receive instant notification when you get a Twitter update, or your chess opponent makes their move, instead of having to manually browse to the Twitter app or chess game to find out.

How does Android compare to a computer for web browsing and email?

Obviously because of the size of the screen and keyboard, the physical experience of using these features initially seems quite different from using a full-size monitor with mouse and keyboard. Once you get used to browsing with a touchscreen, however, and with Android's support for Flash and HTML5, you'll find very few obstacles between you and your life online. Sending emails feels more like sending a text message, to the point where you may have to double-check whether you're doing one or the other.

The same version of Android running on three handsets. Although they look very different, the basic functions are more or less the same. If you find this book talking about a feature that's different from what your own phone offers, check the user manual to find out if there's a way to achieve the same thing on your model. If your phone didn't come with a hard copy of its user manual you'll find a software version (usually a PDF) on the manufacturer's website, or if you hook your phone up to a computer via USB (see p.55) you may find one already tucked away in its storage memory.

Why does the display on my phone look different from the ones in this book?

In Android's early days, Google left the user interface at a fairly rudimentary level and actively encouraged handset makers to add their own customizations. This has resulted in a degree of fragmentation in terms of the way Android looks and behaves on different phones. HTC, for example, has its own Sense interface, while Sony Ericsson has Rachael, and Samsung has TouchWiz. With future releases, however,

Google aims to improve the native user interface enough that handset manufacturers and carriers will no longer feel the need to create their own.

So if all these handsets are different, what software can I expect to find on my new phone?

This too will vary depending on your phone's manufacturer and which native Android applications it has combined with ones developed exclusively for its own brand. The names and interfaces of these applications may differ slightly but they perform much the same functions from one phone to the next. You can expect to see messaging applications including SMS and email, a web browser, camera and camcorder utilities, a music player, calendar, Google Maps, contact lists, a news reader and some basic document readers for Microsoft Office and PDF formats. You'll probably also find built-in applications for the more ubiquitous social networking services such as Facebook and Twitter. Your home screen may have an "app tray" near the bottom of the screen that you can tap to see what you've got to start with, including the **Market** app, which you'll find yourself using quite a lot.

> **Tip**: The **Menu** button may be a physical button at the bottom of your phone, or it may be a "soft" button near the bottom of your phone's touchscreen.

Finding your way around

Is the onscreen keyboard easy to use?

If you have a handset that has a slide-out "hard" keyboard you may prefer to use that for heavy duty typing, but the on-screen, or "soft" keyboard, while a little frustrating at first, is surprisingly easy to get to grips with. The text prediction is intuitive in replacing any typos resulting from the close proximity of the keys, and if you switch to horizontal mode (by simply turning your phone onto its side) the keyboard will expand to fill most of the screen and becomes easier to handle. Custom keyboards are also available from the Market, some of which offer functions such as long-press to select numbers and extended punctuation. **SlideIT** and **Swype** are keyboard apps that offer speedier text entry by

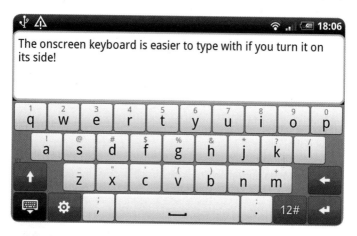

letting you slide between letters without taking your finger off the touchscreen, while **SwiftKey** (see p.211) is a keyboard with an amazing predictive text engine that anticipates what you're going to say next with a worrying degree of accuracy.

> **Tip**: After installing new keyboards you can select them for use by long-pressing the number pad key or any text field. That brings up a list of options, including one called **Input method** where you can select your default keyboard of choice and jump between any you have installed. To change settings for these keyboards, go to in **Menu > Settings > Language & keyboard**.

Can I use a stylus instead of my finger?

You can, but not any old stylus. The touchscreens on most Android™ devices work by recognizing the very specific electrical capacitance of your fingers, whereas most traditional stylus-touch systems tend to be pressure-sensitive. There are a number of conductive "soft touch" styli (often advertised for use with iPhones) on the market and any of these should work a treat if you don't like covering your phone in greasy fingerprints or just prefer using a stylus for fiddly operations like typing on the virtual keyboard.

Does Android feature handwriting recognition technologies?

At the time of writing there are a couple of apps available for handwriting recognition, most notably **Graffiti** and

Touch screen gestures

Android supports a small number of touch gestures that make getting around your phone much easier…

Tap: pretty straightforward, simply tap the screen to activate any app, widget or button, to make selections from menu lists, toggle check-boxes and so on.

Double-tap: basically two short taps in rapid succession. toggles between a zoomed-in and fit-to-screen view in many apps including the photo gallery and web browser.

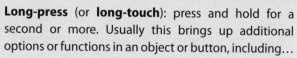

Long-press (or **long-touch**): press and hold for a second or more. Usually this brings up additional options or functions in an object or button, including…

▶ Long-press your phone's **Menu** button (in any app but not on the home screen) to show or hide the virtual keyboard.

▶ Long-press your phone's **Search** button to bring up Voice or Gesture search (if you have them installed).

▶ Long-press your phone's **Home** button to show a panel with your six most recently used applications.

▶ Long-press your phone's **Back** button when using the stock web browser to show your browsing history.

▶ Long-press any text on a webpage to select parts of it and trigger **copy** and **paste** functions (see p.23).

▶ Long-press in any text input field to switch between different keyboards if you have more than one installed, and to choose select, **copy** and **paste** functions.

▶ Long-press any item in a web browser to view options for that item (copy link, save image, bookmark link and so on).

▶ Long-press an app or widget to add it to your home screen. Once it's there, long-press again to move or remove it.

▶ In your calendar or any list such as your contacts or text message archive, long-press an item to show a menu of different options for that item (add event to calendar, delete contact and so on).

Pinch and **spread**: spreading your finger and thumb away from each other zooms in to pictures or text. Very useful when viewing those tiny doll's-house versions of webpages that you get when you first open them up. Pinching, naturally, does the opposite.

Drag and **swipe**: dragging means touching your finger to the screen and moving it around, for scrolling through lists and moving between the pages of an eBook or your home screen. Swipe achieves the same thing but is more of a casual flick and moves things along faster.

These gesture functions can be augmented with a few apps such as Google's **Gesture Search** (see p.213), which allows you to draw letters on your screen to quickly home in on one of your contacts, and the **Open Gesture** and **Oftseen Gestures** apps, with which you can invent your own gestures and assign them functions.

MobileWrite, which recognize simple lower-case letter forms. More advanced script recognition apps are in development, including **MyScript** and **Nuance**. Keep an eye out for them in the Market.

Getting directions in Android – all you have to do is ask.

What about voice recognition?

The Android platform supports voice recognition straight out of the box. Simply press the microphone icon next to the search field and speak your query, or tap the microphone icon on the soft keyboard for voice input entry in any text field. This may not be enabled on your particular handset (some HTC models, for example), but you can download the free **Google™ Search By Voice** app from the Market to enable voice search, and then add a custom keyboard (see p.211) that incorporates the voice button. There's also a handy app called **Voice Command**, which saves your voice to text on the clipboard so that you can paste it into a text field.

Speak your search query clearly towards your phone and you'll be taken to a Google™ search page. Speak someone's name and you'll be taken to your contact entry for that person. From 2.2 you can also use commands such as "Navigate to…", "Map of…" and "Phone…" (or "Call…"), and you'll be taken to the appropriate map or phone function. Useful if you're driving and need to make a hands-free call or get directions.

Tip: Long-pressing your **search** button also brings up the voice search function (or a menu to choose between that and voice command if you have it installed).

How do I copy and paste text?

Not every app will allow you to copy and paste text, and the specifics vary for those that do. If available, selection, copy and paste functions usually start with a long-press (see box on gestures, pp.20–21), or by clicking the **Menu** button (or in Gmail™ and some other apps it's **Menu > More**). Any text input field will let you

The web browser is one of the easiest programs to copy and paste text selections from, but even that can be a bit fiddly.

"[This case] could have implications for all other phone manufacturers which have just announced their phones at Mobile World Congress."

Mobile World Congress is a showcase for every Feb

Ma Ericsson, LG, Samsung and HTC announced new handsets running Android at the show.

"2010 is going to be the year of Android," said Mr Fogg.

Apple announced the legal action against HTC on 2 March.

Legal web

In a statement Apple boss Steve Jobs said: "We can sit by and watch competitors steal our patented inventions, or we can do something about it.

Introducing the home screen

The home screen is the starting point for most things you'll want to do with your phone. Think of it as a similar kind of space to your computer's desktop – it has a few buttons near the bottom for getting to the most needed functions, and a certain amount of real estate up top which you can populate with folders, shortcuts and any number of clever gizmos.

The main difference between your phone's home screen and your computer's desktop is that your phone has multiple home screens, which you can shuffle between by flicking your finger left or right across the screen. On some phones

you can pinch the screen to reveal thumbnails of the lot (left) and move from one to another. Some of your screens may already be occupied by a full-screen widget (a weather report, RSS news reader, SMS messaging and so on). If you don't like this setup, you can move them around or get rid of them altogether and add whatever you like in their place. Simply long-press any item and it becomes moveable: you can reposition it on the current screen, drag it over to the next one, or drag it down to the bottom of the screen to delete it.

Add new items to your home screens by long-pressing on any empty area to bring up the **Add to Home** menu. You'll notice you can also add custom folders and shortcuts to specific app commands in addition to your actual apps and widgets.

At the top of the screen you'll find the Notification bar. This displays a range of little icons to let you know what your phone is up to: on the right are the battery level, various connection states (Wi-Fi, GPS, etc) and a clock, with application-oriented notifications over on the left (updates available, new mail, missed call etc). If you touch the bar you'll find you can drag it down to the bottom of the screen and reveal these notifications in more detail.

If you have an older phone and are missing some of the features discussed here, check out the **LauncherPro** app (see p.202). Other impressive home screen customization apps include **Open Home** (p.205) and **SlideScreen** (p.204).

copy and paste, though; just long-press each field for your options.

What are widgets – and how are they different from apps?

Essentially both widgets and apps are programs that run on your phone. The difference lies in how they are used. An app is a program that you actively start up and use to do something – surf the web, play games, send an email and so on. A widget, on the other hand, is a smaller version of an app that can run from your home screen. For example, a weather widget might be periodically downloading and updating weather information to your phone; a social networking widget might collect together your contacts' updates from Facebook, Twitter and any other services you're subscribed to and show all of these from a single area on the home screen.

> **Tip**: Keep an eye on the number of widgets your phone has running and how often they're set to update, as they could be working away unnoticed in the background, eating up valuable network data allowances and battery power. You can curb this by going to **Menu > Settings > Accounts & sync** and unchecking the **Background data** and **Auto-sync** options.

Just to confuse matters slightly, many apps also have a smaller widget that provides their more popular functions straight from the home screen without the need to open

The Calendar application (above left) is a fully functional calendar, while the Calendar widget (at the bottom of the right-hand screen) just shows you imminent events with basic editing functions (tap the widget to edit the event). At the top of that screen is the Power control widget, which gives you instant access to switching Wi-Fi, Bluetooth, GPS and auto update on or off, and to adjust screen brightness.

the full application. The music-streaming app **Pandora**, for example, contains a widget that can run from the home screen so that you can rate songs and control music-playing options on the fly.

Sync questions

Can I get the contact numbers off my old phone and onto my new one?

As with any phone, you can save the contacts from your old phone to your old SIM and then pop that into your new phone to copy them across. If you have a microSIM, adapters are available for around $5. On your Android™ phone, go to the **Contacts** app (depending on your make and model, it may be called **People** or something similar), press the **Menu** button and select **import/export > import from SIM card**.

Pressing the **Menu** button when in Contacts will present you with import/export options. The **View** button lets you select which kinds of contacts populate your list.

What about my Gmail contacts – can I import them?

If you set up your Google™ account on your phone when you first started using it you'll find that your Gmail™ contacts are syncing wirelessly with your phone without you having to do a thing. You can create groups, new contacts, delete contacts and perform all other contact-related actions, from either your phone's contacts list or your computer via your Gmail account, and (assuming you have an active Wi-Fi or 3G connection) one will mirror the other within a few seconds. If you haven't set up your Google account on your phone yet, go to **Menu > Settings > Accounts & sync > Add account** and select **Google.**

I have a whole load of other stuff that would be useful to sync to my phone...

With varying degrees of success and complexity you should be able to sync anything that's syncable to your Android phone, from your other email accounts and calendars, to your to-do lists, music collection and more. This book has a dedicated section on keeping your devices in sync; shuffle over to p.91 for the full story.

The **Accounts & sync** settings page allows you to set up your phone to sync with your online accounts.

29

App questions

You keep going on about the Android Market – can you tell me more about it?

It's one of the best things about Android™ – an online software store hosting over seventy thousand programs from Google™ and third-party developers. The **Market** app on your phone allows you to browse and install these apps. You can browse by category (games, productivity, lifestyle and so on) and read user reviews. A lot of the apps are free to download; others can cost anywhere between a few cents and thirty or forty dollars. For a more detailed view of the Android Market™ and how to use it, see p.113.

> **Tip**: There's an app for just about everything – if only you're prepared to sift through them to find the most useful ones. The good news, though, is that the second half of this book (from p.133) is packed full of app reviews, so for now you need look no further.

How many apps can I load onto my phone?

Earlier versions of the platform limited app storage to the phone's internal storage memory (ROM), plenty of space for your average user. From 2.2 onwards, however, applications can be installed to an SD storage card (see p.55 for the different kinds of memory in your phone, and p.127 for info on how to do this). In theory this removes any serious limitation on the number of apps you could install, so go fill yer boots!

Can Android run the apps my friends have on their iPhones?

You won't be able to download and run actual iPhone apps from Apple's iTunes Store, but you will find that many apps are developed for both platforms, so the chances are that if you're looking for a particular iPhone app you'll find it (or something that does the same job) for download on the Android Market. Android apps may work slightly differently from their iPhone equivalents and, relatively speaking, Android is a fairly new platform, so some of the major players (IMDB, for example) are only now starting to offer Android equivalents to apps that have been around on the iPhone for a while. That said, it's an exciting time to be an Android user, with new apps appearing at a dizzying pace.

Will every Market app work with my phone?

Probably not; the slowness of some phone companies to update to the latest version of Android means that users of older phones may find themselves left behind as newer apps come out that only support more recent releases of the platform.

Some apps are just badly written or may not work properly with specific handsets. The user review entries are invaluable for saving yourself a lot of time installing duds.

Something else you'll see now and again in the Android Market are apps that will only work if you have "root" access (which means hacking your phone – see box on pp.56–57 for more).

Users of the Android Market are pretty candid about what does and doesn't work for them. Be sure to peruse the comments and ratings for an app before you install it. If they look anything like the ones shown here, the rest of the community has just saved ten minutes of your life that you can now spend playing NESoid (see p.194).

Is there anywhere else I can get apps from?

Because the app market hasn't been locked down and competition is openly encouraged, you'll find a growing number of sites online where you can browse and install apps not currently available on the Market (see p.125).

If I reset my phone or switch to another one, will I have to pay for my apps again?

If you log in to the Android Market with the same Google login as you were using before, you'll see all your previously downloaded apps in the Download section. From here you can re-install any of your apps and any you've already paid for will be free.

Can these apps contain viruses?

Technically, no. When apps are installed they provide a list of their "capabilities" to the operating system, basically a list of all the different functions it will need to access. Once installed, it's impossible for the app to do anything (such as using your phone to make calls or accessing your GPS location) that it hasn't declared in its capabilities. It's worth scrutinizing these permissions that you're granting the application to make sure it's not asking to do anything you'd consider unnecessary (see p.74).

An app's capabilities will be shown to you as permissions which you have to grant the app before you can install it. For more about how this works and why you need to stay on top of it, see the security question on p.72.

Productivity questions

Can I use my Android phone to edit Word and Excel docs?

There are a quite a few document viewers available free in the Android Market™ that'll let you open and look at Office documents of various kinds. If you want to be able to edit and save them, though, your choices are more limited. The paid version of **Documents To Go** is one of the best options currently available (see p.208).

How can I access my Google Docs™ files?

Out the box there isn't a way to do this other than through the web browser, but you can grab a little app called **GDocs** (see p.140) that'll let you sync and work on your Google™ documents, spreadsheets, presentations and so on.

What about making notes and storing ideas?

Take a look at **Evernote** (see p.138) and **Springpad**. Both are awesome ways to create and collate notes, pictures, voice memos, web links – pretty much anything that you want to keep track of or remember – and store them all

in one web location for easy access. Both services provide very usable apps for Android™ as well as a desktop version for your computer, so you can make and view entries from just about anywhere. There are plenty of basic notepad apps, to choose from on the Market (mostly all called **Notepad**, with or without a space) with functions ranging from basic note-taking to colour-coding, tagging, sharing and syncing.

What about a good to-do list?

Got 'em by the dozen! RememberTheMilk.com has an Android app that works with its Pro accounts, but if you use its free account, the free **Astrid** app (see p.136) will sync with it. If you're more a fan of Toodledo .com for organizing your tasks, you can use **Got To Do Lite**, a richly featured task manager that syncs nicely with the online service.

The humble to-do list is one of modern life's nagging necessities. Astrid (above) makes its relentless badgering more appealing by offering friendly encouragement for each scheduled task.

Media questions

Can my Android phone download music directly from the web like my computer can?

Currently you can do this through a number of services including the **Amazon MP3** store/application. You can also use the iTunes-user friendly **DoubleTwist** app (p.160), which can be installed on both computer and phone to sync music between the two devices. If you want to keep using

DoubleTwist is probably the best option for an integrated media player if you're migrating over from iTunes and want a similar kind of experience.

Is downloading music legal?

Yes, as long as you use a legal store like Amazon. As for importing CDs and DVDs, the law is, surprisingly, still a bit of a grey area in many countries, but in practice no one objects to people "ripping" their own discs for personal use.

What could theoretically put you on the wrong side of the law is downloading copyrighted material that you haven't acquired legitimately – and, of course, distributing copyrighted material to other people. A huge amount of music is shared illegally using peer-to-peer applications such as **Soulseek**, BitTorrent clients like **Vuze** or **uTorrent**, and more recently from services like Rapidshare.com and Hotfile.com. With millions of people taking part, it seems impossible that everyone will get prosecuted, though there have been a few token cases on either side of the Atlantic. With new legislation, such as the UK's Digital Economy Bill and similar laws, being implemented around the globe, it seems that all but the most hardened filesharers will become discouraged from engaging in such activities for fear of having their Internet connection cut off.

iTunes and just want a way to sync playlists with your phone, it may be worth looking at **iSyncr** and **mSpot**.

Future Android™ releases look set include access to Google Music, an Android user's equivalent to Apple's iTunes Store, which Google™ is hoping will help further narrow the gap between the two platforms.

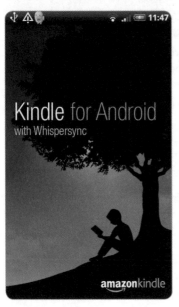

I've bought several Kindle eBooks from Amazon… can I read them on my phone?

Yes, you can, with Amazon's **Kindle** app, free to download from the Android Market™. The app syncs seamlessly with Amazon so that all your Kindle titles are available to read on your phone. Borders has a similar app called **Kobo** for accessing its two-million-strong eBook library.

What about other eBook formats?

There are a whole bunch of other "reader" apps, including **iReader**, **FBReader**, **Aldiko** (see p.174) and **Laputa**, for reading non-DRM-encoded files in various formats including ePub, oeb and fb2 files.

What's this DRM thing you keep referring to?

DRM (digital rights management) is the practice of embedding special code in audio, video or eBook files in order to limit what the end user can do with those files. Some stores and distributors embed DRM into all their wares to prevent them being shared or played using anything other than their own proprietary software.

Can I read PDF documents in Android?

As usual, there is a selection of dedicated free or cheap PDF viewers in the Android Market, including the official **Adobe Reader** and the more feature-rich **BeamReader** (see p.215). PDF support is also included in the multiformat **Documents To Go** reader (see p.208).

Right: BeamReader, a popular alternative to Adobe's offering, isn't free, but includes bookmarking, an invaluable feature absent from most other PDF viewers.

Is there a good way to read comics?

ACV (also know as the **Droid Comic Viewer**, p.172) is a simple, free, lightweight comic and image viewer that'll do everything you need it to. The developer, Robot Comics (robotcomics.net), also has its own comic releases for download from the Market.

Is it good for games?

Absolutely. Developers have moved quickly to show what's possible with the Android platform, and the release of version 2.2 saw massive increases in gaming speed. There's an ever expanding section within the Market dedicated to gaming apps, browsable by category (Arcade & Action, Brain & Puzzle, Cards & Casino and Casual). You can also

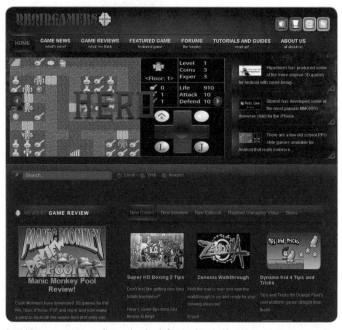

DroidGamers.com is well worth a look for Andriod-related gaming news and reviews, features and forums.

play mobile-optimized Flash games at android-games.net and kongregate.com. For reviews of all the newest and coolest games, visit:

▶ **Droidgamers** droidgamers.com

▶ **Eurogamer** eurogamer.net

▶ **Best Android games** bestandroidgameaward.com

▶ **android games hub** androidgameshub.com

What about podcasts? How can I get those?

Yup, **DoggCatcher** is a fully functioned, paid-for RSS reader and podcast player, while Google's own free **Listen** app (see p.165) is improving all the time from its humble beginnings and may well be a serious contender by the time you read this. If you prefer to manage your podcast feeds from your computer and sync them with your mobile, try **DoubleTwist** (see p.160) or **MediaMonkey**.

... And video? Is there a good all-purpose media player?

Yes indeed, that too! Check out the aforementioned DoubleTwist, and while you're at it, take a look at **Zimly**, **RockPlayer** and, for streaming radio, **Wunder Radio** (see p.166) or **TuneWiki**.

Camera questions

Can my phone take photos and video?

You'll find both a camera and camcorder app in your phone's **All apps** list. What these apps look like and which functions they have will vary, but you should find basic controls for flash, zoom and a shortcut to your picture gallery quite easily.

> **Tip**: More advanced controls will be available from a sidetab, or via the **Menu** button.

Can I use my phone for video calls?

If you have a model with a front-facing camera, then yes. Depending on your contract, you may be allowed to make video calls from your phone for an extra fee. Contact your provider for details. It's also possible to use a third-party service like **Fring** (see p.185) or **Qik** (see p.164) for making video calls over Wi-Fi (see p.51).

Can I upload my photos and video to the web?

Android™ syncs with Flickr, Picasa™, Facebook, YouTube™ and most other places you'd want to share your stuff. From the photo and video gallery, press **Menu** and then the **Share** button ( ) to bring up a list of your current options. See the "Staying in sync" section starting on p.91 for more.

What is augmented reality?

Augmented reality has become a bit of a buzzword recently. It's basically a way of taking location data from your phone's GPS and internal compass and using this to superimpose images or information on the screen when pointing your camera. This information varies from the useful to the utterly ridiculous. A good introduction to the world of augmented reality can be found in **Layar**, which superimposes historical data, fun objects, site-specific virtual sculptures and architectural information on the screen as you point your camera at things when out and about.

One of Layar's featured attractions is a mystery Beatles tour; point your phone's camera at the zebra crossing outside Abbey Road studios and see the Fab Four crossing the road.

What else can my phone's camera do?

App developers have gotten pretty clever when it comes to making full use of your phone's hardware, and the camera is no exception. Photo and video apps are reviewed from p.159, but read on for a handful of other things your camera can do…

Measure distances and heights with Advanced Ruler Pro

This complex and powerful program uses your phone's camera and accelerometer to estimate distances and heights.

You'll first need to calibrate it to your eye level so that the app knows how high off the ground your phone is before

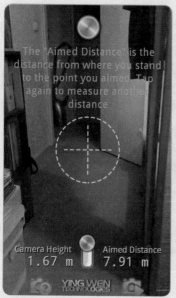

it proceeds. You'll then be able to calculate the height of a building by positioning the crosshair at its bottom and top. Distances and lengths can be calculated in a similar way.

Scan printed pages and get translations with Google Goggles™

Goggles is an impressive multi-faceted application from Google that, among other things, lets you point your camera at a page of text and have it converted into text on your phone.

Google Goggles, attempting to decipher some difficult source material.

You can also use it to point your camera at some text in a foreign language and get an instant translation, or snap a client's business card and convert it into a contact on your phone. See the full write-up on p.137.

Use the camera's LED flash as a torch

Grab the free LED Light app from the Market and get a simple app and widget to control your phone's camera flash. It's an invaluable little program, brighter and less of a battery drain than the plethora of screen-oriented flashlight apps that are available. Older phones may not support this app, but can use an app like **Color Flashlight** to turn the screen bright white instead.

Get price comparisons with ShopSavvy

ShopSavvy (free from, you guessed it, the Android Market) lets you take photos of a product's barcode when out shopping and feeds you instant price comparisons from other retailers.

Connectivity questions

How can I connect using my Android phone?

Android™ has built-in support for Bluetooth and Wi-Fi. From version 2.2 it supports 802.11n, currently the fastest Wi-Fi standard, though your phone's hardware won't necessarily support it. Wi-Fi standards are backwards compatible, so you should have no problems connecting to Wi-Fi networks that support the older 802.11b/g standards. Unless you encounter any specific issues with a particular home network setup, there really is no need to worry about these different standards, as they can generally all coexist quite happily.

You may also have 3G web access via your SIM card and phone carrier. 3G is a data standard used by cellphone network providers to handle the growing data demands of their customers. It's useful when you want to access the web and Wi-Fi isn't available, but depending on your contract you may have a data limit or be charged extra for using this service.

Can I make phone calls while on the Internet?

Yes, if you have access to a Wi-Fi Internet connection. For example, if a friend called you up and needed directions, you could put them on speakerphone while you looked up their location in Google Maps™, talking them through the rest of their journey. Android also supports simultaneous voice and data using the 3G and EDGE data networks, but whether your handset and/or carrier does may be another matter.

Can I "unlock" my Android phone and use another SIM card or network?

If your phone is "locked" to a specific network and you'd like to unlock it, for example if you're travelling abroad and want to save money by using a local SIM card, or if you're at the end of your contract and want to move over to another provider on a pay-as-you-go tariff, the process will be as straightforward as unlocking any other phone.

Before you can unlock your phone you'll need to know a few bits of information…

▶ Your phone's make and model

▶ Your current network provider

▶ Your phone's IMEI code – this is your phone's number plate, usually found hiding behind its battery, or by dialling ***#06#**, or by going to **Menu > Settings > About phone > Phone identity**.

> **Tip**: It's good to have your phone's IMEI code written down somewhere, as in the event of loss or theft you can contact your provider and have them use this number to lock your phone down. It'll also make your phone easy to identify if recovered.

Once you have this information to hand it's a simple case of browsing to one of the many sites that offer unlocking codes. Check out cellunlocker.net, imeisimunlock.com or trycktill.com, enter your information and get the unlock code to enter into your phone. A lot of sites will charge you for the service but surf around a bit and you should be able to find a free one.

Can I use Android to get my laptop online when out and about?

Assuming you have either a Wi-Fi or data connection, Android supports both USB tethering and the ability to set up your phone as a wireless hotspot. Tethering is the process whereby one device connects to the Internet via the online connection of another. So, for example, if you needed to get your laptop online in a situation where no Wi-Fi signal was available, you could connect your phone via USB and employ it as a 3G modem. Set this up from **Menu > Settings > Wireless & networks > Tethering & portable hotspot** and simply select the **Tethering** box (make sure your phone is connected to your computer with the USB cable). That's all

you need to do: Android will handle the rest.

Setting up your handset to act as a wireless hotspot is just as easy. From the same screen, select the **Portable Wi-Fi hotspot** check-box. After a few seconds you

Setting up your Android phone as a portable Wi-Fi hotspot is easier than you'd think.

should see "Android AP" as an available Wi-Fi connection on your computer. You can delve deeper into the settings on your phone for this connection if necessary, to change security settings or change the name of the connection.

What is Bluetooth? What can I use it for?

Bluetooth is a short-range wireless technology separate from your phone's Wi-Fi connection. It allows you to exchange data with other Bluetooth-compatible devices in the immediate vicinity – Bluetooth-enabled computers, hands-free headsets, newer PlayStations and Wii devices, and other phones.

There are plenty of hardware devices that take advantage of Bluetooth connectivity, including a full-size fold-out travel keyboard from freedominput.com. There are also plenty of ingenious apps waiting to make use of your phone's Bluetooth connectivity, including **Torque** for grabbing data and stats from your car's engine, a MIDI controller for musicians called **Midi Pad**, a **Heart Rate Monitor** app (which requires a Bluetooth-enabled chest strap) and the **Bluetooth File Transfer** app (see p.214), which does what it says on the tin.

Can I use my phone overseas?

Shortly after arriving in a new country your phone will alert you to the fact that new phone networks are available, and offer you the choice to connect to one. From then on you

Finding free wireless

These websites will help you locate free wireless hotpots. It's worth checking more than one as none are completely comprehensive…

▸ **Hotspot Locations** hotspot-locations.com

▸ **WiFinder** wifinder.com

▸ **Wi-Fi Free Spot** wififreespot.com

▸ **ZONE Finder** wi-fi.jiwire.com

can use your phone as normal, but check with your provider back home to see what their charges are for making and receiving calls overseas. When it comes to foreign use of web, email, maps and other Internet-based features, you're best sticking to Wi-Fi hotspots where you can get online for free (or pay a reasonable charge for access). In many countries it's possible to connect via the local 3G phone networks, but brace yourself for some hefty data roaming fees when you get back home. If you can stomach the costs, turn **Data roaming** on from **Settings > Wireless & networks > Mobile network**. You may also need to contact your phone company for staff to activate data roaming at their end. A cheaper solution if your phone is unlocked (see p.47) is to purchase a compatible 3G data SIM when you get to your destination and then access networks at the local rate, or to grab one of the SIMs from maxroam.com or gosim.com, which are usable worldwide for a reasonable rate.

Can I use my phone to make VoIP calls?

Check your phone contract's data plan to see whether or not you're allowed to do this over a network data connection. You'll definitely be able to make VoIP (Voice over Internet Protocol) calls over a Wi-Fi connection if you have access to one. VoIP services allow you to connect to other VoIP users for free and to make actual phone calls for a fraction of the cost. You can also use a service like the increasingly popular **Fring** (see p.185) to connect to people on other major VoIP services.

The VoIP world is in flux at the moment with alliances being made and unmade on what seems like a daily basis. **Skype** looks set to start offering VoIP calls to Android users again, after withdrawing their **Skype Lite** app earlier in the year – visit skype.com for further details.

> **Tip:** For cheap non-VoIP international calls over your phone's actual phone line (as opposed to Wi-Fi) check out the free **Rebtel** app from the Market.

Fring is currently one of your better options for making free VoIP calls over Wi-Fi.

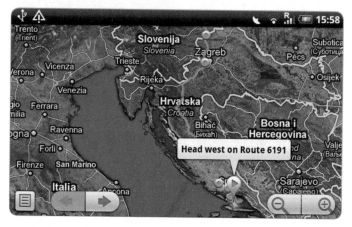

There's a wealth of excellent GPS software and services available for Android but unless you need offline navigation, good old Google Maps can't be beaten.

Can i use my phone as a satnav?

Your phone has a built-in GPS (Global Positioning System) chip, and out of the box (from 2.0), **Google Maps Navigation**™ (p.147) can combine satellite positioning data with network-based map data and provide you with turn-based navigation. There is, however, no offline mode, so you'll also need a Wi-Fi or mobile data connection for it to show you your position on anything other than a blank map.

Can I use these services overseas without racking up a fortune in roaming charges?

It's worth noting that GPS and location-aware features *can*

Offline GPS services like MapDroyd let you download your maps in advance and then get your location over GPS without needing an Internet connection.

operate independently of data roaming. So as long as you use an app with "offline" mapping features (the map data is downloaded as part of the app, and not pulled from the Internet in real-time), you should be able to get a fix on your current location with data roaming switched off. **RMaps** (see p.149) lets you "cache" Google Maps data from areas you know you'll be visiting and use them for navigation later on, while **MapDroyd** (see p.149) lets you navigate around pre-downloaded maps for free.

Alternatively, full GPS software suites such as **CoPilot Live** (see p.148) can transform your phone into a fully functioning offline sat nav without the need for an Internet connection.

Getting technical

Why is my phone stuck with an older version of the Android platform?

With new Android™ releases coming out a couple of times a year it takes manufacturers a while to port the new code to their various devices and user interfaces. If you have an older phone you may find that your phone is stuck a couple of versions back and probably shouldn't expect an update any time soon. Giving your phone "root" access may be a way to add functionality and get a bit more life out of it (see box

on pp.56–57). Alternatively, if your phone's running 1.6 or 2.0 you'll be able to add some of the functionality of later versions using **ADW .Launcher** or **LauncherPro** (see p.202).

The next release of Android (version 3.0) is rumoured to

LauncherPro (left) is a great way to squeeze a little more functionality and panache out of an ageing handset, offering multiple home screens, useful widgets for working with your contacts and calendar, and more.

state minimum system requirements (see box, p.81), making it unavailable to a lot of phone models still on the market, although this is unconfirmed at the time of writing.

SD? RAM? ROM? It's all memory isn't it? So what's the difference?

ROM (Read Only Memory) is used to store your phone's operating system and any apps you have installed. These are loaded into the RAM (Random Access Memory) when needed. Together these two memory chips make up part of the computer that runs everything on your phone.

SD (Secure Digital) is flash memory, similar to the kind found in digital camera memory cards and USB memory sticks (although the card itself is sometimes smaller and not so easy to remove). You can store your photos, backups, music and other files on it like you would with a computer's hard drive. It's much smaller than a hard drive, but less bulky, less power hungry and less likely to break if the device is dropped. Like a memory stick, when your phone is connected to your computer via USB, you can browse the files stored on the internal SD card and move music, photos and other files between the two devices.

Can I use my phone as a hard drive to move files between computers?

Straight out of the box you'll be able to connect your phone to a computer via USB and drag files to and from its internal

When connecting your phone to a computer via USB, select the Disk drive option so that you can access its internal SD memory as if it were an external hard drive or memory stick.

SD storage. With a visit to the Market you'll be able to move files around more effectively within the phone itself using a decent file manager (see p.135). You'll also find programs that let you shift files around between phone and computer via Wi-Fi, FTP and any other way imaginable. There are also widgets available for Dropbox and other popular online storage/backup solutions (see p.109).

Can I use my phone as a touch-sensitive control pad for my Mac or PC?

There are a few apps in the Market that let you use your phone as a wireless keyboard, mouse or touchpad to control your computer. Some of these work over Wi-Fi and some over Bluetooth. USB Bluetooth dongles for PC or Mac can be found for under ten dollars if you want to go down that route.

RemoteDroid is a highly regarded free wireless touchpad app, as is **GRemotePro**. These kinds of apps usually require you to download and install a server application to your computer in order to work, so there may be a small amount of setting up involved, but nothing too complicated.

GRemotePro (right) can be used in a variety of ways to replace or augment your computer's keyboard, mouse, media player controls and more.

What are those crazy square patterns that run through this book?

They're called QR codes, a form of two-dimensional barcode that can contain data such as web URLs, or, in the case of this book, direct links to applications in the Android Market™. If your phone has a camera you'll be able to use the **Barcode Scanner** app (available for free in the Market if your phone didn't come with it preinstalled) to scan these and take you straight to

Getting the most out of your phone's battery

With all the features loaded onto your phone – a bright screen, apps and games, 3G, Wi-Fi, Bluetooth and GPS, to name but a few – your battery can have a tough time keeping up. Here are a few tips on how to give it a helping hand.

▶ **Keep it cool:** Your phone's battery will not hold its charge so well in high temperatures, so keeping it out of your pocket and away from other heat sources will help.

▶ **Switch off 3G:** It's nice and fast but it's a real power hog. If you're not using it, switch it off. Check out **APNdroid**, a useful little app that lets you toggle it on and off without cutting your basic call signal.

▶ **Switch off anything else you don't need:** Your phone may be constantly looking for Bluetooth devices, Wi-Fi hotspots and GPS position. Placing the inbuilt **Power control** widget on one of your home screens makes it easier to toggle these on and off as required. It also lets your switch your screen to a lower brightness level, another great way to save battery juice.

▶ **Update less often:** Just because your phone can pull in Facebook updates, weather reports, stocks and shares, and

the app, ready for installation. The QR code here is for the aforementioned Barcode Scanner app. The cruel irony is you'll need the app before you can scan the code so that you can get the app.

The **Power control** widget gives easy access to most of your battery saving options from one place. (Left to right: Wi-Fi, Bluetooth, GPS, auto-refresh and screen brightness.)

so forth on a minute-by-minute basis, doesn't mean it should. From **Menu > Settings > Accounts & sync** you can select each service you subscribe to and adjust the frequency it updates. You can also use an app like **Tasker** (see p.144) to automate these settings based on where you are, the time of day and other factors.

▶ **Tweak your screen settings:** Changing the time-out settings and screen brightness can help squeeze a bit more life out of your phone's battery. Go to **Menu > Settings > Sound & display** to adjust them. The **Brightness** setting may also have an auto-brightness option you can check, which dims the screen when indoors.

I've heard about Android phones having poor battery life – is this true?

You'll find that after you've "broken in" your phone's battery after a few charges its capacity will improve greatly. If you're

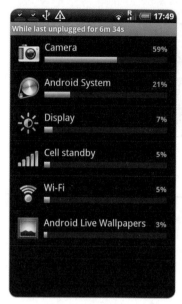

still having battery issues there are a number of tweaks you can make to conserve power. See pp.60–61 for some tips on battery use.

Menu > Settings > About phone > Battery > Battery use will give you an invaluable insight into which functions are chewing up your phone's battery charge. If you're concerned that something is running your phone down all the time, place a shortcut to this page on one of your home screens and check every now and again to find out which function is the culprit.

I've heard that I can install an "app killer" to improve performance and get more life out of my battery. Should I do that?

The short answer is no. There's a lot of debate about applications you can use to stop other applications running in the background, such as the much-touted **Advanced Task Killer** (see p.128), and how running these programs will help save your phone's battery power. These claims are, however, based on a popular misconception about the

It's tempting to select every running task in an app killer to free up RAM and speed up your phone, but generally you should just use it to nip problem apps in the bud.

way the Android platform handles your phone's memory. Application managers are useful if you have a program that seems to have crashed or isn't responding properly, but you won't see any performance improvements from using them to force-quit programs running in the background. See pp.128–130 for a more detailed explanation.

How can I back up my phone?

Assuming you have a Gmail™ account, your emails and contacts will already have an online backup. Specific files can be backed up over USB (p.107), or via **Dropbox** (see p.109), and your apps can be backed up using the **Astro** app (see p.135). If you're looking for a complete backup of your phone's data, SMS messages, calendar, settings, shortcuts, alarms and so on, try **MyBackup Pro** (see p.227).

What is "root access" all about?

Android may be an open-source platform, but once it's on your phone, neither the manufacturer, the carrier nor Google want you messing with it. Still there are reasons you might want to "root" or hack your handset and unlock access to the core operating system.

Why would I want to root my phone?

It allows you to install custom ROMs (so called because they replace the data in your phone's ROM memory), basically tweaked versions of Android for your phone that can add speed, stability and new functionality to outdated models. For example, the option to install apps to the SD memory rather than the phone's RAM only appeared officially in Android 2.2, but some custom ROMs had this feature a long time before.

Root access also enables your phone to run some apps that require deeper access to your phone's hardware, and allows you to cherry-pick the best custom widgets and user interfaces from other phone manufacturers.

Some of the functionality you can achieve by rooting may already be available in your phone's own custom UI, or through future updates to Android, but it's a crafty way to supercharge an older handset if the manufacturer has been slack in keeping it up to date.

What are the risks?

Well, at best you'll probably void your warranty and not receive any further technical support from your carrier. At worst you'll "brick" your handset – it'll stop working altogether. You'll also lose the ability to get automatic over-the-air updates from your phone's manufacturer.

You should also be aware that even if you root your phone successfully, some performance improvements may mean its processor has to work harder, possibly shortening its lifespan or draining more battery power.

So how do I go about it?

Depending on your handset and the Android version you're running, the method will vary, but a quick web search including the words "root" and the model of your phone should yield plenty of results. Tread carefully though, and always read the comments on any blogs or forums you visit to check how successful other users have been.

Obviously if you do this, you'll be on your own in terms of technical support. If, after considering all the risks, you're certain you want to go ahead, you should always back up all of your data and contacts first using **Astro** (see p.135) or **MyBackup Pro** (see p.227).

Internet questions

What web browser does Android ship with?

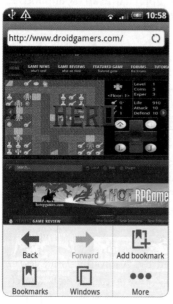

The Android web browser isn't much to look at, with only an address bar at the top of the screen, but it's lightning fast and will display pretty much anything you can throw at it. Press the **Menu** button for more options.

The stock Android™ browser is based on the same open-source WebKit engine as used by Google's Chrome™ browser. It's pretty snappy for general use, but if you require more advanced web-browsing features, like native bookmark syncing, check out **Dolphin** (see p.152) or **Opera Mini** (see p.153), both available for free from the Android Market™. There's also a mobile browser in the works (code-named Fennec) from Mozilla.org, developers of the popular Firefox browser. It's currently still at the testing stage (see p.154 for a look at the pre-release version) but a final release should be available soon.

Does my phone offer fast Internet access?

If you're within range of a Wi-Fi network, as found in homes, offices and cafés, and across some entire cities, then your Internet access will typically be pretty speedy; not quite as fast as with a top-end Mac or PC, but not a long way off.

If, on the other hand, you're out and about, away from any accessible Wi-Fi networks – walking down the street, say, or sitting on a bus – then you'll need to use a mobile network connection (3G or EDGE) to access the web. A 3G connection won't be as impressive as that experienced over Wi-Fi, but it should be good enough. (For more on the various flavours of cell network connection, see the box on p.67.)

Another factor to consider when out and about is your own speed of travel. If you're on a train or in a moving car, you might find that your phone's connection speed is slower than when you're stationary. This is because it's having to accommodate a constantly shifting relationship to the nearby signal masts that it's connecting with, making it hard to maintain a constant and coherent stream of data to and from the Internet.

Will all websites work in Android?

Android's built-in web browser supports Flash and HTML5, so in terms of the kinds of content you can view (YouTube .com for example – see below), you'll find that your web

YouTube™ in full-screen mode within Android's built-in browser. Flash content plays in much the same way as you'd expect from a computer browser.

experience is pretty much equivalent to that of a desktop computer, albeit a bit smaller.

Will I be able to use the BBC iPlayer?

The BBC has put in a lot of work to ensure their iPlayer service is compatible with Android devices. If your phone is running 2.2 or later – and you live in the UK – you'll have no problems accessing iPlayer, or indeed any other Flash-based web content, but you'll need to grab the **Adobe Flash 10.1 player** from the Android Market if it's not already installed.

Phones with older versions of the platform should download the **myPlayer** app (p.163) instead to get around

EGDE, 3G ... what's all that about?

Over time, the technology used to transmit and receive calls and data from mobile phones has improved, allowing greater range and speed. Of the network technologies widely available at present, 3G (third generation) is the most advanced, allowing Internet access at speeds comparable to home broadband connections (at least when stationary). 4G devices are also now beginning to appear, providing even faster and more stable access.

EDGE (an acronym for Enhanced Data rates for GSM Evolution), which is sometimes referred to as "2.75G", offers a theoretical top speed of 236 kilobits per second (kbps); in practice, however, users have experienced connections as slow as 50kbps – like an old-fashioned dial-up connection. Your phone should be able to use either technology and will connect to whatever is available in your locality. One advantage EDGE has over 3G is that it is much more economical in terms of battery power.

any potential lack of Flash support. You'll need a decent Wi-Fi connection to handle the amount of streaming data.

What do I do if my mobile Internet (EDGE/3G) stops working?

You could try enabling and then disabling Airplane mode (press and hold your phone's **Power** button for a menu which includes this option). Or, if that doesn't work, reboot your phone.

How come some websites look different from how I'm used to seeing them?

A lot of sites will auto-detect your phone's browser and redirect you to a mobile version of their site. These are usually pared-down sites with the key features clearly

Same site, different look: the mobile view (left) and classic view (right) of lifehacker.com. It's not as interesting to look at, but the mobile site allows you to get straight to the content without bells and whistles getting in the way.

displayed. You should still be able to access all of the site's content but the interface may not be what you're used to. Viewing the regular version of the site on such a small screen usually involves a lot of zooming in and scrolling around, so if a mobile version of the site exists and you're not redirected automatically to it, you'll probably find it by directing your browser to m.sitename.com, mobile.sitename.com or sitename .com/m.

Will Android work with my email account?

Yes. As you'd expect, Android has excellent Gmail™ support, and, in the rare case that your phone doesn't come with one, there are email clients available for working with POP3, IMAP and Microsoft Exchange email services (see p.209). Other popular sites like Yahoo! also provide their own apps that integrate closely with their web and email services.

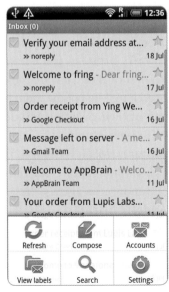

The Gmail app gives instant access to the more useful elements of the service. If you need access to synced third-party accounts and other features you can probably find them hiding behind the **View labels** tab.

Gmail will sync seamlessly with your Android phone. Delete a contact or message from your phone, and it'll disappear from your Gmail contacts list online. Add one, and watch it appear at the other end.

It's possible you could encounter problems when setting up a work email account, depending on the policies of your network administrators. The only way to be sure is to ask. For more on setting up and using email, turn to p.93.

> **Tip:** Don't forget that you can also access your email through the web browser.

I like to chat – are there any IRC clients?

More than you'll ever need! **Android IRC** is a popular choice if you're happy to pay a few dollars, but check out the free version of **AndChat** first and see if it does everything you need it to. Most of the main IM chat clients have an Android app of their own, but **eBuddy Messenger** and **Meebo** (see p.158) are handy IM clients that hook up with multiple accounts (MSN, Facebook, Yahoo!, AIM, ICQ, Google Talk™ (which your phone may already have installed), MySpace and more). As always, these apps are all available from the Android Market.

Security questions

Does Android present any security risks?

The Android Market™ is not heavily moderated by Google™, but it's been documented that one or two apps (out of thousands) have been removed for attempting to harvest users' financial data. At present the risks are minimal, with any vulnerabilities quickly patched up by Google; still it seems only a matter of time before malware becomes just as prevalent on this platform as any other.

But isn't Android based on the Linux OS? Linux can't get viruses, can it?

It's true that Linux isn't a popular target for viruses, and that the way the Android™ platform allows apps only certain permissions means it would be very difficult to write a virus or malware that could do damage to a phone's operating system. It's also true that malicious apps cannot install themselves on your phone without your approval, but there's still the risk that an app can be installed which seems to behave normally while using the permissions you've granted it in ways that you wouldn't normally endorse.

I've noticed a few anti-virus programs on the Market – do I need one?

Anti-virus programs for Android don't offer much of a

security benefit in and of themselves but may incorporate other useful security tools, such as the facility to remotely lock the phone or check installed programs against lists of known malware. Because the only way malicious software can currently get onto your phone is by you actually agreeing to install it, your best line of defence is to be very careful about what you install, be wary of unrecognized email attachments, always check the user reviews and permissions before you install an app, and only use apps from trusted sources.

> **Tip**: It's worth remembering, too, that your phone could transmit viruses between other devices (someone else's computer and your own, for example) in much the same way as any other storage device can. So if you routinely connect your phone to more than one computer, take the same precautions you'd take with any other portable storage (external disks, memory sticks and so on) and use the computer to virus scan any files you're moving to and from the phone.

What are these "permissions" and how do they work?

When an app is installed it will provide a list of its "capabilities" to the operating system, basically a list of all the different functions it will need to access. You'll see these listed as "permissions" on a page as an orange-coloured list for you to read through before you go ahead and install the app.

Always check the permissions when installing apps. If it seems like a program is asking you to let it do more than you think it needs to, do a bit of research before you OK it.

Once installed, it's impossible for the app to do anything (such as using your phone to make calls or accessing your GPS location) that it hasn't declared in its capabilities. That said, there's always a risk that some apps could declare capabilities beyond what they'd legitimately require, potentially opening up some worrying security or privacy issues. It's worth scrutinizing these permissions that you're granting the application to make sure it's not asking to do anything you'd consider unnecessary.

Tip: Permissions for your already installed apps can be seen by going to **Menu > Settings > Applications > Manage applications** and tapping on an app. It's educational to take a look at some of the applications you know and trust to see what kinds of permissions they need in order to operate.

How do I tell whether an app's permissions are legitimate?

Up to a point you can use a degree of common sense: does that shoot-em-up game you're about to install really need access to your contacts list? If in doubt, do a quick web search and see if anyone seems to be ringing alarm bells about that particular app.

Just to confuse things, sometimes an application may request permissions that seem unreasonable but are necessary for it to function properly. For example, a media player may need to monitor your phone calls so that it knows when to put music on hold for the duration of a call.

If you want to know specifically which services your apps can access, use **aSpotCat** (free from the Android Market), which gives you a greater level of detail than your phone's own application settings page.

aSpotCat lists your installed apps by permission, so you can see, for example, all the apps that access your GPS location or use services like SMS that can cost you money.

Is it safe to use my phone to connect to public Wi-Fi hotspots?

There's a small risk with any Wi-Fi capable device that someone could be snooping in on data travelling via an open network. You should apply the same common sense when using public Wi-Fi networks as if you were using a laptop: unless you absolutely have to, avoid using Internet banking or any other service that requires you to enter sensitive personal data.

Are there any other risks?

Perhaps the biggest risk – as with any device as portable as a phone or laptop – is that someone could steal it and access your private data. If you're worried about that possibility, the easiest line of defence is to set an unlock pattern and SIM card lock (see below).

So how do I lock my phone?

Out of the box, there are a couple of options. A pattern lock is the most straightforward, but you can also use a SIM lock. Both of these options can be found under **Menu > Settings > Security**.

To set up a pattern lock, check the box that says **Require pattern** and then select **Change unlock pattern**. You'll see a square of nine dots. Draw a continuous line between the dots in a pattern that's complex enough to not be

It's amazing how quickly your finger will remember a fairly complicated pattern like this, but if you decide to go for something really elaborate it might be an idea to draw yourself a little diagram for reference.

immediately obvious – not, then, the big "Z" that's used for demonstration in the phone's manual – but simple enough to remember. You'll then be prompted to confirm your pattern by drawing it one more time. Now, when your phone goes to sleep or is switched off, the next time you go to use it again you'll be presented with an unlock screen that requires you to draw that same pattern before you can access the home screen.

Setting a SIM card lock can be done from the same security settings screen. Select **Set up SIM card lock** and then check **Lock SIM card**. You'll be prompted at this stage for your existing PIN. If you don't know it, check the documentation that came with your phone to see if it's listed anywhere, or call your network provider and they'll provide you with it after verifying your identity. Once your SIM PIN is set up, anyone trying to use the phone will be required to enter this four- to eight-digit number. After three wrong attempts the SIM will be locked and you'll need to contact your provider again for a Pin Unlock Code (PUK), or buy a new SIM card and start again.

What else can I do to help protect my data?

Apps like **WaveSecure** (see p.143) can give you an extra layer of security by providing the facility to lock down your lost or stolen phone, erase the SD card or remove certain permissions. They can also help locate your phone and then restore much of its contents if recovered. WaveSecure costs $20 for a yearly subscription (although the app itself is free), but if you're only after one or two of its features (the ability to locate your phone via GPS, for example) you can probably find them more cheaply in another app or as part of a mobile anti-virus suite such as **Lookout** (see p.228).

However, the best way to keep sensitive data safe is to keep it somewhere other than your phone: on your home

WaveSecure offers peace of mind in return for an annual subscription.

computer or backed up to a remote server (using a service like Dropbox, p.109).

Should I be worried about the kinds of information I'm sharing from my phone?

As with any device that connects to the Internet, it's worth paying close attention to which elements of your online presence are being shared beyond your real-life social circle. Facebook, Twitter and other social networking services make it very tempting to update the world with anything from where you're staying on holiday to your innermost thoughts. You can amend the privacy settings so that only your friends and family can see anything but the most basic details; but it's still safest to assume that anything you share online is accessible to far more people than you'd expect, perhaps including exes, future employers and cybercriminals.

All of this is even more important if using your phone to connect with GPS-enabled social networking services like **Foursquare** (see p.157), as anyone resourceful enough can use a service like this as a springboard for accessing any information about you that's publicly available, as well as to track your location with the same degree of accuracy as your own phone can.

Tip: Bluetooth can be used to transmit data between your phone and other devices up to around 30 feet away, so unless you're actively using it, switch it off (this will save battery power, too).

How can I be sure my personal information is deleted when I sell my old phone?

It's worth considering what kinds of personal data your phone may still contain if you decide to donate, sell or throw it out at some point in favour of a newer model. You'll probably want to wipe certain information, but unfortunately it's a little more complicated than selecting files and telling the phone to delete them. Deleting files in this way only reallocates the space they occupy as empty – ready to be overwritten if that space is needed – but the files themselves are still there and can be recovered using the right tools.

Recellular's wireless recycling pages offer advice and instructions for wiping information from your old phone.

It is possible to permanently erase sensitive data so that it's rendered unrecoverable. Check to see if there are instructions in your phone's manual or on the manufacturer's website. If not, you can try the data erasing instructions available from tinyurl.com/2f4ue4.

Buying options

Which model? Where from?

So you're ready to jump in and get yourself an Android™ phone. Which brand should you get? What kind of contract do you need? Where should you buy it? The next few pages will help you figure out what your options are.

What should I look for?

It's always best to do some research of your own before buying into a product or service, especially for something as complex and multifunctional as a smartphone. Read reviews online and check the forums at androidcommunity.com for the make and model you have in mind to see if there are any potential issues you should know about. You can also compare reviews at specialist technology sites, like the ones below:

▶ **Tracy and matt** tracyandmatt.co.uk

▶ **Tech Radar** techradar.com

▶ **Pocket Now** pocketnow.com

▶ **Recombu** recombu.com

Which version of Android?

At the time of writing it is rumored that the release of Android™ 3.0 will carry with it certain minumum system requirements. Any phone not meeting these hardware requirements won't be receiving any further updates after 2.2. If you're concerned about your new device being forward compatible it's worth taking a quick browse around the Internet to find out what the current situation is, and if minimum specs have indeed been officially released.

That said, there would obviously be a substantial price step between an older but perfectly serviceable phone running 2.2 and an all-singing, all-dancing one running Android 3.0, so weigh up your options and ask yourself if you really need to be on the cutting edge.

The main areas to consider when choosing a handset are:

▶ **Brand:** Each of the different manufacturers – Samsung, Sony, HTC, et al – have their own take on the Android experience and this can vary between phone models too. If you can visit a store in person, it's well worth playing around with phones made by all the major companies so that you can get hands-on experience of their user interface.

▶ **Screen size vs portability:** Large screens are obviously nicer to look at and better for watching video, but does your phone still fit in your pocket? For forward compatibility with future Android versions, you should look for models with at least a 3.5-inch screen size.

Some handsets, like this one from Motorola, slide open to reveal a full keyboard and trackpad. If you plan on using your phone to send a lot of emails or you're an IRC addict it's a feature you may find appealing.

▶ **Keyboard:** Are you happy to do most of your typing with a virtual (soft) keyboard or do you need a physical keyboard that slides out from under the screen? It may be worth trying out both in a store, and figuring out whether the extra bulk of a hard keyboard is something you want to carry around everywhere you go in exchange for potentially faster typing.

▶ **Other hardware:** How good is the phone's camera? What kind of flash does it have? Does it have a front-facing camera for making video calls? Does it have an HDMI (High Definition Multimedia Interface) video output or other useful connections? You'll be the best judge of which concerns are your priorities, but it's worth investigating what the options are within your price bracket.

▶ **RAM:** Measured in megabytes (or MB), this is the memory that your phone uses to run the Android platform and any applications you're using. For current phones, 512MB is more than enough.

▶ **Processor (CPU) speed:** Measured in Gigahertz (or GHz), this is how fast your phone can process information. Higher is better, but for forward compatibility you should look for a minimum of 1GHz.

▶ **Android version:** Obviously higher is better but don't expect your new handset to be running the latest version, as handsets running much older versions of the platform are still on sale.

Where to get a phone

Once you've decided on your preferred phone model, you can choose to sign up for a contract with a network provider (in which case the cost of the phone will usually be subsidized or waived completely) or buy the phone outright and use a pay-as-you-go SIM. It's worth considering how much you use your current phone and whether you really need to be tied in to an often expensive and lengthy (12-, 18- or 24-month) contract, or if you'd like the relative freedom of pay-and-go.

Signing up for a contract

When choosing a phone contract there are some obvious factors to consider: What's the monthly cost? How many call minutes do you get? How many free texts? What's your monthly data allowance? Are there any extras? Deciding which deal to go for depends on how you're likely to use your phone: are you more of a talker or a texter? If you know you're going to be mainly on the Internet, or intend to make extensive use of your new phone's navigation abilities and other web services, then it's worth shopping around for the best 3G data deal. Unlimited data deals, once the norm, have become increasingly rare.

The major network carriers have branches in most major towns and cities, so you can easily walk in and pick up a phone on the spot. There are also one-stop shops like the Carphone Warehouse and Phones4U in the UK, and Walmart in the US, where you can peruse offers from various carriers in one place and pick the one that suits you best.

In the UK:

▶ **Carphone Warehouse** carphonewarehouse.com

▶ **Phones4u** phones4u.co.uk

In the US:

▶ **Walmart** walmart.com

▶ **Best Buy** bestbuy.com

It's also well worth shopping online. Apart from the carriers' own websites, there are some phone comparison sites that resell the same package deals you'd get in-store but with substantial discounts or cashback incentives that could cut the cost of running your phone by up to a third over the life of the contract.

Authorized online agents are paid commissions by carriers to bring in new customers and offer a simplified credit application process and often give discounted phone prices.

In the UK:

▶ **The Phone Network** thephonenetwork.co.uk

▶ **Mobiles UK** mobiles.co.uk

▶ **One Stop Phone Shop** onestopphoneshop.co.uk

In the US:

▶ **Point** point.com

▶ **Let's Talk** letstalk.com

▶ **A1 Wireless** a1wireless.com

If you're in the US and want to get out of your existing contract it may be possible to sell on the remaining months of your deal through one of several online reseller programs:

▶ **Cell Trade USA** celltradeusa.com

▶ **Cell Swapper** cellswapper.com

Or, in the UK:

▶ **Cell Swapper** uk.cellswapper.com

Buying without a contract

If you want to skip taking out a long-term phone contract

and use a pay-as-you-go service or rolling monthly contract, it pays to shop around for the best price on a new handset. Try a price-comparison agent such as, in the US:

▶ **Google™ Product Search** google.com/products

▶ **PriceWatch** pricewatch.com

In the UK, price-comparison agents include:

▶ **Kelkoo** kelkoo.co.uk

▶ **Shopping.com** uk.shopping.com

Some online retailers tend to make quick deliveries and offer a reliable returns service, including the best-known of all:

▶ **Amazon US** amazon.com

▶ **Amazon UK** amazon.co.uk

Used/secondhand phones

Buying a secondhand Android™ phone is much like buying any other piece of used electronic equipment: on the one hand you could find a bargain but you might just as easily land yourself with an overpriced paperweight. If you buy a handset that's less than a year old, it should still be within warranty, so you'd be able to get it repaired for free if it doesn't work properly – even if the phone in question was purchased in a different country.

Whatever you buy, it's good to see it in action before parting with any cash, but remember that this won't tell you everything. If a phone's been used a lot, for example, the battery might be on its last legs and soon need replacing, adding indirectly to the cost.

If you buy on eBay, you'll get loads of choice and a certain level of protection against getting sold a dud. Be sure to read the auction listing carefully and don't be afraid to ask the seller if you're unsure of anything. You'll often find people selling unwanted brand new handsets that they've received as part of an ongoing network contract. This can be a great way of snapping up a bargain, but be aware that the handset you're buying may well be locked to that network and will need to be unlocked if you want to use it with another (see p.75).

Insurance

Now you've got your shiny new phone it may seem a bit scary walking around with a flashy gadget worth hundreds of dollars in your pocket, and the insurance packages offered by your network carrier may suddenly start to look like a good idea. If you're trying to assess whether or not insurance is worthwhile it's best to take a long, hard look at yourself and determine whether you're the kind of person who's always losing or breaking things, or if you're the kind of person who likes to keep everything in plain sight and pristine condition. If you're the former of the two then insurance may be for you.

It pays to shop around, though, as the coverage offered by your phone provider probably costs over the odds compared with what you can get from third-party insurers. In the UK, visit insureyourmobile.co.uk or insurance4mobiles.co.uk and explore your options. In the US, visit ensquared.com for a helpful comparison of the best phone insurance deals. Policies vary in price depending what's on offer, so consider how important the following are to you:

▶ Are you covered for calls made by someone else if your phone is stolen?

▶ Are you covered for accidental damage and loss as well as theft?

▶ Are you covered if you go abroad?

▶ Will it cover damage or loss of phone when used by other family members?

▶ Are your mobile phone accessories covered?

▶ Will you need to pay an excess, and if so, how much?

Policies can also vary depending on whether you're on a pay-as-you-go or monthly contract. It's worth checking too whether your provider will send you a secondhand or refurbished replacement phone instead of a new one.

Tip: As an alternative to getting a specific insurance policy, check whether your home insurance covers your phone, or whether it could be added to the policy for a small addition to your regular payment.

staying in sync

Staying in sync
Email, calendars and more

Now that you have a phone that's capable of performing a lot of the same tasks as your computer – email, web browsing, social networking, playing music and video – wouldn't it be great if you could get everything to work across the two devices so that you could move from one to the other without having to manually shuffle files and settings around every time? Well, with Android™ you can do exactly that.

Depending on how you already use your phone and computer, you'll find some level of synchronization of email and other online accounts will be up and running without much effort on your part. Other things, like your bookmarks and calendars, may be more clunky to set up, but still doable with a little tweaking and some apps from the Market. There are a number of ways to approach synchronization between your phone and other devices, but by far the easiest is to keep your data remotely stored via "the cloud" (aka the Internet) and sync everything with that. This may sound daunting to set up, but for the most part all you need is a Gmail™ (aka Google Mail™) account.

All-in-one solutions

If you don't have or don't want a Gmail™ account, or simply want to sync stuff directly between your computer and phone, there are other options available to you. These will vary in complexity depending on your setup – Microsoft Exchange users, for example, will have a fairly easy time of it, while owners of some handsets will find they have a "sync mode" which presents itself as an option when connecting to their computer via USB (using this will usually involve downloading and installing a small server program on the computer from the phone's SD card – visit the manufacturer's website for more details).

Syncing with Microsoft Exchange

Setting up your phone to use Exchange ActiveSync with your Exchange emails, calendars and contacts is simple. Look to **Menu > Settings > Accounts & sync > Add account** and choose **Exchange ActiveSync**. From there just enter your email address and password (if you experience problems, select **Manual setup** and enter your server details). If your older Android™ handset doesn't have this facility already, there are several apps that can sync to an Exchange server, **Touchdown**, **RoadSync** and **ContacsCalendarSync** being solid examples.

> **Tip**: For an all-in-one online sync solution, take a look at the service offered by memotoo.com – they'll sync just about anything with anything. A limited free account is available, with a premium service costing $18 a year.

Third-party sync solutions

If your phone doesn't come with its own built-in USB sync option, there are a few apps on offer that will facilitate the syncing of contacts and calendars. One of the more comprehensive options available is the **Missing Sync** app, which can sync calendars, notes, text messages and all kinds of files between your phone and computer. The app is free but the corresponding program for Mac or PC (markspace .com/products/android) will set you back $40.

> **Tip**: If you're an Outlook user and want to sync with a Google™ account, but need more robust capabilities than those offered by the Google Calendar Sync option (see p.100), including full contacts, calendar and mail syncing, it may be worth investigating a subscription to Google Apps Premier Edition, which allows you to use the **Google Apps Sync for Microsoft Outlook** application. Visit tinyurl.com/yc78f89 for more details.

Mail & contacts

Email without Gmail

Your phone's own dedicated email client can be used to grab mail while leaving it on the server for your computer to pick up later. To set up your email accounts from within your mail client, go to **Menu > (More) > New account** and add as many Microsoft Exchange ActiveSync or POP3/IMAP email accounts as you like. Once you have your email accounts set up, browse to the **Receive settings** and you'll be able to set a maximum size limit for mails to download (useful for avoiding large attachments if you're on a limited data plan). You should also make sure that the option **Delete mail on server** isn't selected, otherwise once it's been downloaded to your phone it won't be available to your computer. (If your computer stays on all the time, you may want to set your email client up to leave mail on the server too, so that your phone can pick it up, although at some point you'll need to manually delete emails if your mailbox has a size limit.)

There are a few alternatives to the stock Android™ email client: try **MailDroid** or **K-9 Mail** (see p.209), both available free in the Market.

So what exactly is Gmail?

Gmail™ is Google's webmail service, equivalent to those offered by Yahoo! and Hotmail. You're probably familiar with the concept of webmail, where your emails are stored online (as opposed to downloading them through an email client and keeping them on your computer). The main advantages of webmail are that you can access your email from anywhere in the world by simply logging in through a web browser; your mail and contacts are safely backed up and accessible in the event your computer is lost or damaged; and you get stacks of storage space for your emails. The only real disadvantage is that you need Internet access in order to refresh them.

Tip: Once you've got a Gmail account, you can use the same login to access other Google™ services like Calendar, Documents, Groups, Picasa™ and many more.

Can I use Gmail in parallel with my existing email setup?

If you prefer downloading your email and viewing it offline through an email client like Thunderbird or Outlook, you can simply tell Gmail to pull in your emails from other accounts while leaving them on the server for your email client to pick up, giving you the best of both worlds. You can even use your existing email addresses to send emails from within Gmail.

Getting a Gmail account

You can set up a Google account in a couple of minutes from your phone or from your computer's web browser. On your computer, Visit gmail.com and click the **Create an account** button. The next page will ask you for your name, the name you want to give your account, your chosen password, and other standard login-related stuff like your location and a security question in case you forget your password. Once you've filled in the form, hit the **Create my account** button and you're done.

Tip: You may want to uncheck the **Enable Web History** and **Stay signed in** boxes when setting up your Gmail account if you're concerned about privacy or if using a shared computer.

Setting up Gmail on your phone

Your Add Account screen will be pre-populated with some familiar options. Tap on any of your synced accounts to select which elements (mail, calendar and so on) you'd like to sync.

When you switched your phone on for the first time you will have been prompted to enter your Gmail account settings, so you may have already entered them. If not, head to **Menu > Settings > Accounts & sync** and tap the **Add account** button. You'll see options to toggle various popular web services (Facebook, Twitter, etc) alongside one for Google. Tap on Google and follow the steps to enter your details. You can set up a new Google account from scratch from this screen, too.

So how do I sync my emails?

Assuming you already have a Gmail account, that's all you need to do. Your Gmail messages (and those from other linked accounts) will be instantly accessible from the Google Mail™ app and one will mirror the other (within a few seconds, assuming you have an active Wi-Fi or 3G connection).

What about contacts?

You'll also find that all your Gmail contacts have quietly found their way into your phone's contacts list. Now you can create groups, new contacts, delete contacts and all other contact-related actions from within your phone's contacts list or from a web browser and they'll sync automatically.

> **Tip**: For easy contact syncing between Thunderbird and Gmail (and hence your phone), check out the **Google Contacts** and **gContactSync** add-ons. You can also use Mozilla's new Contact add-on which syncs all your web-based contact lists (Facebook, Gmail, LinkedIn and more) with the email client.

Can I move my existing contacts and emails into Gmail?

Yes. If you're using another webmail service, all you need to do is log into gmail.com and click on **Settings** (top right of your browser window), then click the **Accounts and Import** tab and at the top you'll see the option to import contacts from your Yahoo!, Hotmail, AOL or any other webmail account. You can also set up Gmail to pull in email

Settings

| General | Labels | **Accounts and Import** | Filters | Forwarding and POP/IMAP | Chat | Web |

Import mail and contacts: Import from Yahoo, Hotmail, AOL or other webmail or POP3 accounts.
Import mail and contacts   Learn more

from your other email accounts from this page. If you have multiple email accounts, this is a great way to access them all in one place. You'll still be able to use your desktop email client as normal, but you'll have duplicates going to your Gmail account.

> **Tip**: At the bottom of the "Send mail as…" section of Gmail's Accounts and Import settings tab, you can select a radio button to reply from the same address to which the message was sent. This will let you reply to emails from any of your email addresses, even from your phone, without switching to another account.

If you have contacts stored in your computer's email client, Outlook or Thunderbird, say, you can save or export them to a CSV file (most email clients can do this). Save the CSV file in DOS format and you can import it into your Gmail contacts list by logging in to gmail.com, pressing the **Contacts** button and clicking **Import**. Once imported to your Gmail contacts, they'll sync over the air to your Android phone.

If using Apple's Mail and Address Book, you can easily keep your contacts synced with your Gmail account; open **Address Book**, go to **Preferences**, click on the **Accounts** tab, check the **Synchronize with Google** box and then enter your account info. You can then sync the two by clicking **Sync Now** from the Sync menu in the menu bar. Note that you can only sync with a single Google account.

My Gmail contacts have synced to my phone – and there are hundreds of them!

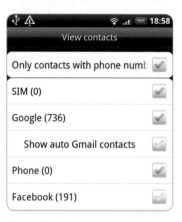

Bitten off more than you can chew? Pare your contacts list down by selecting which sources your phone syncs with.

The annoying thing about Gmail's contacts sync is that it'll pull in every single email address that's in your Gmail contacts list – basically everyone you have ever emailed. The simplest way to resolve this is to go to **Menu > View** on your phone contacts list and, if your phone has it, select the **Only contacts with phone numbers** option.

Another workaround that may work on your handset is to go to **Menu > Settings > Sync Groups** and choose which groups to sync with (you can set up and edit these groups from your Gmail account). This is an area where every handset seems to have a different trick to get it behaving properly. If none of the options above are available to you, do a web search for your handset's model name along with "Gmail contacts sync" and you'll find a solution if one exists, along with some similarly frustrated users.

Calendars

Keep it in the cloud

By far the easiest way to get your Android™ phone's inbuilt Calendar app to sync with any other calendars you already have is to get those other calendars syncing with your Google Calendar™. Your Google Calendar will then sync automatically with your phone over Wi-Fi without any effort on your part.

Tip: With any of the options below, you'll find it easier to export your existing calendars to your Google Calendar and then sync your calendar program to that, rather than the other way around. Once you have this set up you won't notice any difference from how you would normally interact with your calendar.

Syncing calendars with Outlook

Google Calendar online (and subsequently your phone's calendar) can also sync with Outlook, using the **Google Calendar**

Google Calendar Sync takes the pain out of syncing calendars with Microsoft Outlook.

Sync program, available from tinyurl.com/22yq2m. Once downloaded and installed on your computer, simply enter your Google™ account login details and select **2-Way sync**.

Syncing calendars with Thunderbird or Sunbird

Mozilla users can download the **Provider for Google calendar** add-on. This allows you to view and edit your Google calendars directly from Sunbird, or Thunderbird's **Lightning** calendar. Once installed,

To get your Google Calendar's full address, head to its **Settings** page and click the button for the appropriate format.

right-click in the calendar area and choose **new calendar**. Select **On the network** as the calendar's location, and on the next screen, **Google Calendar** as the type. In the **Location** field you'll have to paste in your calendar's full address, which you can find in the settings area of your Google calendar by clicking the green **ICAL** button.

Syncing calendars with iCal

Mac users can sync iCal calendars with Google Calendar by going to **Preferences > Accounts** in iCal and entering your Google account info. You'll need to then go to **Delegation** and select the particular calendars you want iCal to access.

Once you're in sync with Google, you'll be syncing with your phone.

If you're not running the current Mac OS, check out the instructions for syncing earlier versions: tinyurl.com/56byzz.

Bookmarks

Can Android synchronize bookmarks with my computer's web browser?

Ironically, while Google™ does offer a bookmarking service at google.com/bookmarks, it hasn't gotten around

to implementing any kind of sync between this and the built-in Android™ browser as yet. There are a few workarounds you can set up. It's possible to sync both Chrome™ (click the wrench icon and select **Set up sync**) and Firefox (using the **GMarks** add-on) with Google Bookmarks to get

Bookmark syncing in Android is currently a bit of a mess. Until it's ironed out, you'll find apps like Transmute will help smooth things over a little.

all your bookmarks synced up in one place. Then you can use apps like **GoMarks** or **Transmute** to pull these into the Android browser. If you're using the **Dolphin** web browser (see p.152), you can sync directly with Google Bookmarks.

> **Tip**: Android's built-in browser doesn't currently support bookmark folders, so if you have lots of bookmarks you may want to pare them down before you import them to save trawling through an endless list every time you need to access one.

Alternatively, if you already use bookmark syncing from xmarks.com or delicious.com, these services have their own apps on the Market that will sync with your phone.

Another option is to start using the Opera web browser on your computer and use **Opera Mini** on your phone (see p.153). The Opera Link feature enables you to sync bookmarks between the two.

If you simply want to import your bookmarks from Internet Explorer, Firefox or Chrome, use the **MyBookmarks** app from the Market.

Syncing social networks

Facebook and Twitter

Social networking is a doddle to set up on an Android™ phone. Depending on your handset, chances are it came with **Facebook** and **Twitter** apps built in; it may also have prompted

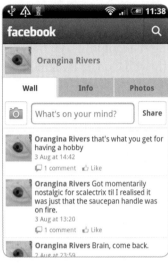

The official Facebook app gives you immediate access to most of the site's common major features.

you to set these accounts up when you first used your phone; and it may even have already sneakily combined Facebook photos and contact details with people already in your contact list.

If you don't already have them installed, the official apps for these and other social networking sites are available for free from the Market, along with a dizzying array of third-party equivalents. It's best to start with the official apps and then try some of the others if they offer extra features you feel you're missing. Once installed, you can set how often you'd like the app to sync with your online account, and which kinds of data you'd like to see. You'll find detailed settings within the app itself under **Menu > Settings**, with more general sync settings available from your main **Menu > Settings > Accounts and sync** screen.

Tip: Don't forget that you can still access these sites (and your Gmail™ and Calendar) from your phone's web browser. Most networking sites have a mobile or touchscreen-optimized version which you may prefer using over the dedicated app.

Sharing stuff

One of the great things about using the Android platform for social networking is how easy it is to share stuff. Any apps you install that allow you to upload content to the web (not just social networking sites, but photo sites like Flickr, note-taking services like Evernote, and so on) will integrate with the share function available in apps where you create content. Usually this appears as an option when pressing the **Menu** button, or by long-pressing an item to bring up a list of actions (sometimes also displayed as 🖐️).

For example, from your phone's photo gallery, press the **Share** button (or **Send**, depending on the app) and you'll

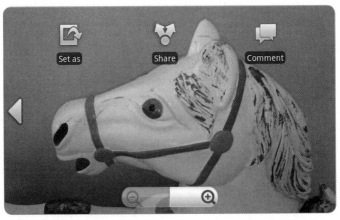

Most apps that handle or create media (sound, video or photos) will give you a **Share** option from the **Menu** button. From there you can upload the file to any accounts you have set up.

be presented with a list of different locations where you can send the picture, such as your Facebook photo album, your email app (as an attachment), Tumblr account, or any other location you have the relevant app for. The same is true for, say, a voice memo or PDF file. The locations on offer will change depending on the type of file you're trying to share and whether or not the sites in question can handle it. You can share a photo with your Flickr account, of course, but if you select an MP3 to send, you won't see Flickr as an option.

Combining your social networks

Wonderful as it is being able to access all these different streams of information coming in from all over the web, it's a pain to be constantly jumping between webpages and apps. Enter the snappily named social networking aggregators, a group of apps that pull everything together in one place. Your phone may well have shipped with one – Sony Ericsson's is called **Timescape**, while Motorola has **Motoblur** and HTC offers **Friend stream**, for example. Any of these will draw in newsfeeds, status updates and other information from all your synced accounts and give them to you in one long list.

> **Tip:** If you're looking to try a third-party social networking aggregator, check out **Buzz Deck** or **TMN Pond** (see p.155).

Syncing computer files

Simple file management over USB

The most straightforward way to move files between your phone and computer is to connect the two together with the USB cable that came with your phone. Your notification bar should automatically drop down at this point to reveal your connection options, but if not, drag it down and select **Disk drive**. Now on your computer you'll be able to see your phone displayed as a removable disk (as far as your computer is concerned it'll look like a memory stick). Double-click this and you'll be able to browse the folders and files on your phone's SD card (but not its operating RAM) in the same way as you'd browse the files on your computer.

You'll find quite a few folders there already. Some of these will have come with your phone, some backup files, possibly a PDF manual, that kind of thing. There'll also be folders called "MP3" or "music", where your music lives; a "media" folder, where you can place any custom ringtone, alarm or notification sounds (you'll need to create a sub-folder for each type you want to add, eg **media/ringtones**, so that the phone will know where to pick them up); a "My Documents" folder; and a DCIM (Digital Camera Images) folder, which stores any photos or video you've taken using your phone's camera.

You can drag files to and from the phone, delete and copy, and perform any other standard file actions. The folders mentioned above should be the only ones you need to bother with. It's best to leave the others be as they can hold data and settings relating to some of your apps. However, if you see a folder with the name of an app that you're certain you've uninstalled, you can safely go ahead and delete it.

Tip: Why not copy the entire contents of your SD card over to your computer on a regular basis anyway? It'll serve as a backup in case you delete something important or lose your phone.

Syncing music and media

If you feel that rummaging around in your phone's SD memory isn't for you, you'll be pleased to hear that iTunes-like syncing of media files can be yours, thanks to the **DoubleTwist** app. Once installed on both your phone and

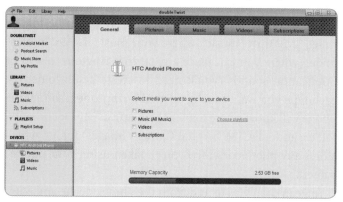

DoubleTwist in action on a PC, a one-stop hub for syncing your media.

computer, it takes the form of a standard media player which will start up as soon as you hook up your phone via USB. From here you can sync playlists, videos, photos and podcasts, preview and buy MP3s from the Amazon MP3 store, subscribe to podcasts and browse (but not install) apps from the Android Market™. DoubleTwist will update its media library from your iTunes or WMP playlists and offers a rudimentary media player of its own, although you may prefer to retain your existing setup for actually playing music on your computer.

Tip: You can also use Windows Media Player (from version 11 onwards) to sync files with your Android™ phone. Simply connect your phone in **Disk drive** mode (see above) and, on your PC, click the **Sync** tab. You can drag music or videos into the tab area to queue them up and then press the **Start sync** button to copy them to your phone.

Syncing remotely over Wi-Fi

The easiest way to get files to and from your phone without physically connecting it to your computer is to set yourself up with a Dropbox account. Download and install the desktop program from dropbox.com on your computer and enter your email address and a password. You can install **Dropbox** on as many devices as you like or, if you prefer, just use the web interface. Once up and running Dropbox places a folder shortcut on your computer's desktop (on

Awesome Drop presents a novel way to get files onto your phone via your computer's web browser.

your phone you'll have to manually place the app on the home screen). Now, any files you place in the folder will upload to the dropbox .com web servers and will appear in the Dropbox folders of any other devices that have it installed. As well as being a neat way to mirror stuff from one device to another, it's also a painless way of keeping an online backup of your important files. A basic account is free and includes 2GB of storage, with more available if you upgrade to one of the paid Pro versions.

An alternative to Dropbox is **Awesome Drop**, a free service that requires no login. Install the app from the Market and then point your computer's web browser to labs.dashwire .com/drop. Here you'll see a big red rectangle with a four-digit number in it. Start the app on your phone and enter that number when prompted. Your browser will now display a green rectangle that you can drag files onto. These files will appear in a folder called "drop" on your phone (you'll need a file manager like **Astro**, see p.135, to be able to access this folder directly), or you can get to the files from the Awesome Drop app window.

apps for everything

The Android Market

It's all about the apps

Pretty much everything you can do with your phone – from playing games or keeping up with Twitter, to remotely managing your business or editing Office documents – is achieved with an application or its related widget. As you'd expect, your phone will come pre-installed with enough features to make it usable – email, your web browser, contacts list, Google Maps™ and so on. But, once you've mastered the built-in applications for these basic functions, you'll probably want to start installing third-party software for a whole range of other purposes.

This is where the Android Market™ comes in. It's your one-stop shop for almost all the Android™ software currently available (with the exception of the Android platform itself). Some of these apps are free, while others cost a few dollars. Once you decide on an app, so long as you're connected via Wi-Fi or 3G, you can have it downloaded and installed in a matter of seconds.

Using the Android Market

You don't need to connect to your computer to shop for apps: the Market is right there on your phone. If you can't see its icon on the home screen, press the **Menu** button and select **All apps** to bring up a list of all the apps currently installed. There'll be quite a few there already, listed alphabetically, so scroll down till you find the **Market** app. You may find yourself heading to the Market quite a lot when you first get your phone so it's worth placing it on your home screen (see p.24).

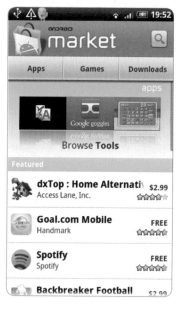

Browsing for apps

Tapping on the **Market** app opens up a screen like the one to the left. The bottom half of the screen consists of a scrollable list of fairly random "featured" apps, while the top half offers basic navigation and a search bar. The **Apps**, **Games** and **Downloads** buttons allow you to browse the Market, taking you to

The Android Market. Get your virtual shoes on, we're going shopping.

sub-categories such as **Multimedia** and **News & Weather** in Apps, or **Arcade & Action** and **Brain & Puzzle** in Games. Once a sub-category is selected you can choose between **Top paid**, **Top free** and **Just in**, or simply scroll down through the seemingly randomized list. Alternatively, you can tap on the magnifying glass button at any point to bring up the keyboard and tap in a search term, giving you a scrolling list of apps that meet your criteria. You won't get much info at this point, just the title of the app, the name of the developer and the price, together with a star rating indicating its popularity with users.

Installing a free app

Select any app and you'll be taken to a screen showing more detail: a couple of lines about what it does, how much memory it'll take up on your phone, and some screenshots that you can click on for a closer look. Click the **Comments** tab to find user comments and ratings (pre-version 2.2, you won't have a Comments tab – just scroll down the page to see the app's reviews).

> **Tip**: It's worth reading through a few of the user ratings as they'll often give you some indication of any problems the app may have on certain handsets, or if it's just plain not worth bothering with.

Tapping the **Install** button at the bottom takes you to a new screen outlining which services and functions of your phone the app will have access to. Give this a quick once-

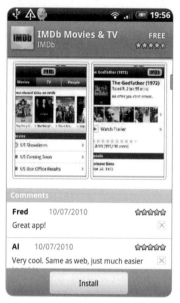

A typical installation page for a free app, in this case the IMDB Movies & TV app.

over (see p.72 if you're not sure why) and click **OK** to install the app. Depending on the size of the file and your connection speed, it should download and install in a few seconds. A small animated ⬇ will appear in the notification bar while it's downloading, changing to a tick ✅ once the app is installed. Dragging down the notification bar reveals a message confirming the app has been installed. Tap on this message to set the app running if you want to try it out straight away. From there on, your new app can be found in the apps list (**Menu > All apps**) or can be placed on your home screen for easy access (see p.25).

Reviewing your downloads

If at any point you want to check which apps you've downloaded, visit the Market, click on the aforementioned **Downloads** button, and you'll see a list of all the apps you currently have installed. Select one and you'll see buttons

If you have second thoughts about your review, you can take it back with the click of a button.

to open or uninstall the app at the bottom of the screen, and the opportunity to give it a star rating and post a comment about it at the top. Comments appear almost instantaneously in the Market alongside any other reviews. If you decide you'd like to withdraw your comment, press the **Menu** button and select **Clear my review**.

Installing a paid app

Sooner or later there'll be a paid-for app on the Market that you want to get your mitts on. You can check out a free trial first, if there is one, but the risk of wasting money on a dud is pretty low, thanks to the Market's 24-hour refund policy (see p.119). Installing paid apps follows much the same process as for a free app, but with an extra few steps the first time around.

First, instead of the **Install** button at the bottom of the app's screen, you'll see, naturally enough, a **Buy** button. Tapping

Google Checkout

If you already have a Google account for Gmail (and you should – see p.94), setting up a Google Checkout™ account is a simple process of entering your credit or debit card details. Google Checkout will then act as an intermediary, handling your Android Market payments for you and passing these charges on to your card. It's a free service that can be used with an increasing number of online retailers and means you don't have to keep setting up new accounts or handing your card details out all over the Internet.

this takes you to a Google Checkout™ screen which, first time around, will ask you for your credit card details. You can enter these here or, preferably, take a minute or two out to set up a Google Checkout account on your computer (see box).

Once you've entered your details you'll see a message that the transaction is being

Google Checkout takes a couple of minutes to set up, but it beats entering your card details every single time you buy an app.

authorized. The first time you use Checkout, your phone will ring at this stage (either your Android™ phone or your land line, whichever number you entered when you were filling in your details). There will be a friendly robot at the other end of the line who'll ask you some personal details in order to verify your purchase. Answer the robot's questions nicely. That's it! You can now start using the app. Meanwhile you'll get a confirmation email sent to your Gmail™ account.

If, after checking it out, you decide that the new app isn't quite your cup of tea, you can return to its page (via the **Downloads** tab in Market) within 24 hours of making your purchase, where you'll find an **Uninstall and refund** button in the bottom right of the screen. Press this button to say goodbye to the app and get your money back. A message sent to your Gmail account will provide confirmation.

Not what you were looking for? If you're quick you can get your money back and try something else.

Updating apps

Looking at your apps list in the **Downloads** section of the Market, you may notice that updates are available for one or more of your apps (you'll also periodically receive messages in your notification bar to this effect, so don't feel that you have to keep checking). Just tap the **Update All** button at the bottom of the screen and they'll be queued to update without any need for you to intervene further. If you're running version 2.1 or lower, however, you'll have to manually select and update each app.

> **Tip**: You can also set individual apps to auto-update in the background. Go to the app's page and check the box at the top to allow automatic updates.

Other ways to browse and install Market apps

Should you find the search and browsing functions offered by the **Market** app a little too limited, it's also possible to browse and install apps from the relative comfort of your computer. As you'd expect, there's a whole universe of Android™-devoted websites out there, and many of the geeky tech review sites have regular roundups of the best apps.

▸ **Recombu** recombu.com/apps/android

▸ **Gizmodo** gizmodo.com/tag/androidapps

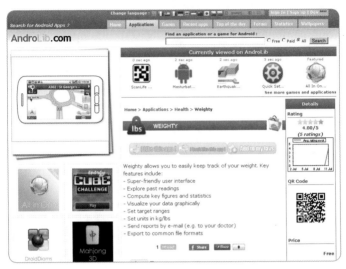

Androlib is a more convenient way of interacting with the Android Market, offering comments, ratings and feature details alongside download stats and suggestions for similar apps.

▶ **Andronica** androinica.com/category/google-android -applications

▶ **Lifehacker** lifehacker.com/tag/android

▶ **Know Your Cell** knowyourcell.com/app-reviews/android-apps

▶ **Android And Me** androidandme.com/category/applications

Many sites publish a QR code along with the review (see p.57). Simply point your phone's camera at your computer screen and, using the **Barcode Scanner** app, you'll quickly be taken to its install screen.

You can also browse the Android Market™ directly from your computer at android.com/market, although you can't install anything or read user reviews, so the site's usefulness is somewhat questionable. You can actually get much more information from sites like Androlib and Cyrket, which present the standard Market information along with QR codes, user reviews and download stats.

▶ **Androlib** androlib.com

▶ **Cyrket** cyrket.com

AppBrain

Androlib and Cyrket are great when it comes to browsing the Market on a bigger screen, but what if you could take that one stage further and actually install these apps directly from the computer? Well now you can. Install the **AppBrain App Market** and **Fast Web Installer** apps (they'll both pop up if you search for "AppBrain" in the Market) and start them. You'll need to log in to the AppBrain App Market app using your Google™ account settings and give your approval for the Fast Web Installer to do its thing.

Once you've set this up you can browse to appbrain.com on your computer and start installing apps. The site is very straightforward: you can browse apps by category, get recommendations, see what's new and so on. When you find an app you like the look of, click the **Install** button. A pop-up window will show the apps permissions (see p.72) for you to approve. Click **Install this app** and it will instantly

As well as uninstalling apps via the AppBrain website, you can also tap on the little red X in the phone app to remove a listed app.

download and install on your phone. You can also uninstall apps from the website by clicking on **My Apps**. From here you can click **Cancel Install** for apps that you've installed via the site, or **Uninstall** for other apps. Firing up AppBrain on your phone, tap **Manage my apps > Sync with AppBrain** to see a list of pending uninstalls. Tapping **Perform installs** will set any queued installs or uninstalls in action.

For installing paid-for apps you'll still need to hop over to your phone to confirm your payment credentials, but for browsing and installing free apps it doesn't get any simpler.

Non-Market apps

The Android Market™ offers more apps than you could ever possibly need, but there are still some apps that for one reason or another aren't available in the official store. This

Slideme.org, one of many new sites offering their own take on the Android Market experience. If you're a developer who can't get their apps on the Market, or if you're a user who doesn't want to go through Google Checkout™, this could be what you've been looking for.

could be because they're incompatible with your handset or Android version, because the app isn't available in your part of the world, or for any number of other reasons. There are, however, other outlets springing up online where you can download and install apps, many of which aren't available in the Android Market at all.

Tip: When looking at paid apps, shop around between download sites and the official Market, as you may find the app you want is available cheaper or even for free. Be aware that these won't carry the same ratings and review system that comes in Android Market, so there's no guarantee of their stability.

Installing non-Market apps

Many of the sites below have their own Market-like apps that allow you to install stuff in pretty much the same way as the official one. Alternatively you can download the .apk installer files direct to your computer then transfer them to the main directory of your SD card. You'll need to get hold of the **Apps Installer** app from the Market. Run the installer and click on the app you want to install.

▶ **AndAppStore**
andappstore.com

▶ **Andspot** andspot.com

▶ **GetJar** getjar.com

▶ **Handango**
handango.com

▶ **Phoload** phoload.com

▶ **SlideMe** slideme.org

If you have **Astro File Manager** (see p.135), you can drop the .apk file onto your SD card, browse to it from within Astro, tap on the file you want to install and select **Open App Manager**. Hit the **Install** button from there and you're done. You can also move files to your backup folder and then install from Astro's **Backup** tool as if you were restoring a saved app.

Technical stuff

The ins and outs of using apps

There are so many apps in the Android Market™ and elsewhere online that it's tempting to download each and every one that seems remotely interesting and/or useful. You may have plenty of space on your phone's SD card, but it's still worth being choosy about which apps you invite to the party. You don't want any guests hogging all the food so that others go hungry, disappearing upstairs and snooping through your things, or sticking around after the party's over. This section will help you manage your guest list, so you don't end up crying on the metaphoric stairs.

Apps and phone performance

Automatic app management

Strip away the exterior and your phone works much like a computer: apps being the programs you run on it. On a computer, if you try to run too many programs at the same time, it struggles to juggle them and may begin to slow down. One of the Android™ platform's strengths is its ability to multitask like a computer – to have a whole bunch of stuff happening in the background while doing something else in the foreground. Which is great, but it's easy to forget if you've just been browsing the web – when you suddenly decide to return to the home screen and open up a game of chess, and then take some pictures with your phone's camera, and then check your Facebook messages – that all these separate apps remain running in the background. On your computer you can see which programs you have open at the bottom of the screen, but how do you know what's currently running on your phone?

Fortunately, you don't need to worry about this too much. Android manages applications and memory in such a way that if a running app isn't currently in use it lies dormant in the phone's memory (RAM) without using any extra battery juice. If it gets to a point where memory is needed for some other task, Android will simply free up as much as it needs by quitting long-dormant apps. It may also pre-load certain background apps and functions into memory but for the most part you can ignore these (see p.128).

Moving apps to your SD memory

Currently, some handsets running Android 2.2 let you move some of your apps to run from the SD memory instead of the phone's operating memory. You may find yourself wanting to do this at some point if you have a lot of apps installed and start to run out of space for new ones.

Moving an app to the SD card is as simple as pressing this button. Want to move it back? Next time you look, this button will say **Move to phone**.

From **Menu > Settings > Applications > Manage applications** tap on an app and, if it's available, you'll see an option to move it to the SD card. A small part of it (a "stub") will remain in the phone's RAM so that the app can function properly, and any widgets that are part of the app will stop working. Officially, it's not possible for you to manually move apps back and forth to the SD card. Your phone would make this decision for you based on available memory. Even if your handset supports it, the capability for an app to be moved to the SD card has to be included in the installer by its developer, so may not yet be available in all apps.

Apps to manage other apps

Task killers: one app to rule them all

A task killer is a small app that you can use to selectively close (kill) other apps on your phone. If you have one of these installed, you'll be able to see that a surprising number of applications seem to be running in the background and it's

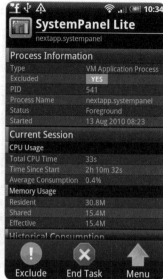

Advanced Task Killer (left) and SystemPanel (right) are two popular task management apps which have free versions on the Market.
But do you need them as much as you think?

tempting to routinely kill as many of these as you can in the hope of making your phone run a bit faster. In fact, it costs the phone as much power to hold "nothing" in its memory as it does to hold actual data, so using one of these programs to constantly kill apps in an attempt to reclaim resources is largely a waste of time, and may actually be causing you more problems than it's solving – you may miss notifications, alarms or email updates, or be forcing the phone to reload regularly used apps back into memory all the time instead of

The Manage applications page in Settings contains detailed information and all the control you need over an app in one place.

just leaving them dormant for when they're needed.

But while task killer apps aren't really necessary for managing phone's memory usage, they do have their uses. If you have a program that's crashed or isn't behaving properly, an app like **Advanced Task Killer** will give you a handy shortcut to force-quit and reload it, which usually solves the problem. The same thing can be achieved, however, by going to **Menu > Settings > Applications > Manage applications** and scrolling down to the app you'd like to quit. Selecting the app takes you to a detailed screen with all kinds of information, including a button to **Force Stop** and one to **Uninstall** the app altogether.

Certain apps may

continually run in the background unless you deliberately quit them. If there's an app that you're convinced is running your battery into the ground, you can use a task killer to regularly nip it in the bud and see if things improve. There are also several resource meter apps on the Market, such as **SystemPanel** (see p.218), which combines a task killer with the ability to monitor individual apps' long-term resource usage. Handy for troubleshooting a slow or laggy phone.

Most of the task killer apps on the Market include an "ignore list" option, which you should use to specify which apps won't close when you blanket-kill all your running tasks. Usually this is achieved by long-clicking an app's name and clicking **Add to ignore list** or the equivalent.

Tip: Some task killers will automatically ignore Android's system apps, but if yours doesn't, you should add the following to your ignore list. These, plus anything starting with ".com", need to be allowed to run so that your phone behaves itself properly: Alarm clock, Bluetooth share, Browser, Calendar, Gmail™, Market, Messaging, My uploads, Package installer, Settings, Voice dialer and Voice search.

Application backup utilities

Because your contact lists and calendar events and email are synced with your Google™ account online, there's no need to back these up, but sometimes it can be useful to have a backup of your apps. You may want to temporarily uninstall

Astro File Manager – the Swiss Army knife of the app world – makes backing up and restoring apps a doddle.

an app to make more room on your phone's internal memory, or return your phone to its original state and start again. There are a few apps that will do this for you, but **Astro File Manager** (see p.135) is one that you're more than likely going to have other uses for, too. Once you've backed up your apps to the phone's SD storage, you can save them to your computer via a USB connection (see p.107).

Start Astro and go to **Menu > Tools > Application Manager/Backup**. Select the apps you want to copy and tap the **Backup** button. Tapping across to the **Backed Up Apps** tab at the top will display your available backups, which can be reinstalled.

> **Tip**: For a more comprehensive backup solution that includes you SMS messages, phone settings and other data, look to **MyBackup Pro** (see p.227).

essential
apps

QR codes for apps will take you to the app on the Android Market™, while standard product barcodes give you the option to hook up with **Google Shopper™** for a price comparison or perform a more general web search on that product.

Barcode Scanner

Not the most glamorous app to start with, perhaps, but one you'll find absolutely indispensable (you'll even be able to use it to scan the codes in this book). Point your phone's camera at any kind of barcode and let this app do the rest. There are a few barcode apps on the Market in various flavours, but this one is fast, lightweight and very easy to use. Look for Barcode Scanner by ZXing Team on the Android Market™.

Astro gives you all the tools you need to manage files and apps on your phone. Tapping on a file brings up options for opening the file, while a long-press will summon a menu of options, including viewing details, editing, sending, setting images as contact icons, setting music as ringtones, and more.

Astro File Manager

If you plan on using your phone for anything other than making calls, chances are you're going to end up with a lot of files and folders rattling around on the SD card. A good file manager is essential for navigating around this stuff and Astro is one of the best you'll find. As well as regular file maintenance (copy, paste, move, delete, etc), you can make zip files, back up, uninstall and reinstall apps, kill problem apps and processes, and set up an FTP connection over a Windows network. The free version has unobtrusive ads, absent in the $3.99 Pro version.

Astrid arranges your task list in order of priority. It'll also plug in to **Locale** and **Tasker** (p.144) to send you reminders based on your location. So that you'll literally remember the milk when you walk past the supermarket.

Astrid

This friendly task list works wonderfully as a self-contained to-do manager. It lets you set priorities and assign tags, durations and notes to a task, and other standard to-do operations. Where it really shines, though, is that it syncs both ways with your cloud-based task list at rememberthemilk .com. Once you've set your tasks, Astrid tenaciously but jovially prompts you to deal with them at the appropriate time, offering encouragement with lines like "Do it, and you'll feel better." Thanks, I feel better already.

Goggles is surprisingly accurate, but works best with man-made stuff like landmarks, artworks, book and DVD covers, products and text. It's not so good with nature and animals just yet.

Google Goggles™

An ingenious app that lets you search the web by taking pictures. Simply point your camera at something and Goggles will attempt to tell you what it is. When out and about, it will use your phone's GPS location and internal compass to provide links to local businesses and points of interest, which pass along the bottom of the screen as you turn to face them. Pointing the camera at a CD or book cover will take you to that item in a Google™ search. You can also use it to scan and convert pages into editable text, or point it at some text in a foreign language for an instant translation.

Evernote integrates nicely with your phone's share functions. Hit **Share** or **Send** from your camera and most other apps and you'll find the option to send the file you're working with to Evernote without even having to start up the app.

Evernote

Evernote looks like a humble note-taking service, but beneath its surface lies a powerful web-based capture tool. Register for a free account at evernote.com and the app will let you send text and audio notes to yourself, upload photos, scanned text and other files, tag them and access them from anywhere via your web browser. Any writing in images you upload gets transcribed into searchable text. It's a neat way to keep all your ideas, reminders and notes in one place. It integrates with free desktop apps for PC and Mac and there's also a paid account option offering more storage space.

gUnit Converter Lite is free, although a full ad-free version is available for $0.99 and includes support for user preferences.

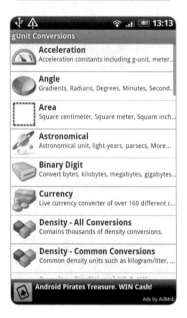

gUnit Converter

An all-in-one converter for just about anything you could ever need to convert, plus a whole load of other stuff you'll probably never need to convert (unless you're an astrophysicist or thermodynamics engineer, in which case you can probably do all that stuff in your head) but is kind of cool to have access to anyway. You know, just in case. It also includes a live currency converter.

Looking for a dedicated live currency converter? Try **Currency Converter** or **Exchange Rates**, both free from the Android Market.

As well as working with basic text documents, GDocs lets you view and edit your Google Spreadsheets.

GDocs

One thing that may be missing from your phone when you first get it is a simple notepad. There are plenty available for free on the Market, but where GDocs stands out is that it allows you to sync notes with your Google Docs™ account. You can use it to view, search and edit existing documents, too, though it's not a fully fledged word processing app.

If integration with Google Docs isn't important to you, take a look at **AK Notepad**, which lets you create basic notes, label them, pin them to your home screen, share them and set reminders. **Note Everything** is also worth a look.

Shazam is pretty acccurate for less obscure songs with a melody, but the more wayward your tastes are, the less luck you'll have.

Shazam

Hey, what's that song they're playing on the radio? Want to know what you're listening to? Point your phone's mic in the direction of the music and **Shazam** will listen to it for a few seconds and get back to you with the answer. It'll also link to the song on the Amazon store and YouTube™ videos, provide discographies, grab tour dates and more.

The free version allows you five searches a month, while the £2.99 version gives you unlimited searches and a few extra features. A similar deal is offered by the **SoundHound** app. Give both a test spin and see which works best for you.

Touiteur takes tweeting to the next level with all sorts of useful features arranged in a clear, functional design.

Touiteur

Competition is fierce at the top when it comes to Twitter apps, but Touiteur has more than one advantage over the others. It's easy on the eye, fully customizable and the premium version (a snip at €1.99) has some great widgets. Touiteur has too many well-thought-out features to list here, but where it really stands out is its use of threaded conversations, making it easier to figure out what someone's tweet was in response to. Tweeting is quick and simple with a decent widget in the free version, and a drop-down bar you can access from anywhere within the app to start typing.

WaveSecure can send automated backups to their remote servers, so that in the event that you do have to wipe your phone, your data can be restored later on, if the phone is recovered.

WaveSecure

WaveSecure is an all-in-one mobile security application. For the cost of a \$19.99 yearly subscription you get the ability to completely lock down, trace the location of, and even remotely wipe your phone and its SD card if lost or stolen.

A designated "buddy" from your contacts lists can be chosen to receive notification if your phone is compromised. Their contact number will then show on the locked screen of your phone, so that anyone who finds it can get in touch with them.

With an almost overwhelming array of functions at its disposal, Tasker is an app for the technically minded tweakmeister in your life. It also works with plugins for the similarly versatile **Locale**.

Tasker

Tasker is a powerhouse of an app that can automate functions on your phone, based on criteria like your location, the time of day, the phone's orientation, and so on. Once you figure out how to program it, you'll be able to set your phone to open your media player automatically when you plug in your headphones, switch your home screen to a different scene when you arrive at your office, go into silent mode between certain times of the day, and carry out just about any combination of other actions your phone can perform. It's available for £3.99 from the Market.

navigation apps

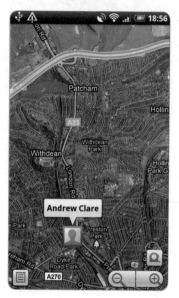

Google Maps™

Maps has been a Google™ product for some years now, and the Android™ app takes full advantage of its ever expanding functionality. Among its many features you'll find GPS support and full search for businesses, locations and addresses anywhere in the world. You can get directions by car, walking or public transport, and view switchable layers for traffic, terrain and satellite views. You can also tap on a location to get more details, read reviews or place a phone call to the address if it's a business, and get a 360-degree street view. It also accepts voice commands (see p.22).

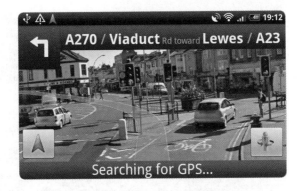

The many faces of Google Maps. Satellite view (far left) superimposes map data over beautiful satellite imagery. Google Places (left) is a quick search hub for local businesses and amenities, while Navigation (above) offers a fully functional GPS sat nav.

The integrated **Google Maps Navigation** (beta) provides sat nav-like turn-by-turn navigation (for voice command functionality, download one of Google's **TextToSpeech** language packs). **Google Places**™ displays places to eat and drink, ATMs, gas stations and places of interest nearby. **Google Latitude**™ shares your location with friends.

The only snag is that it needs Internet access to do any of this, so unless you're on an unlimited data plan you'll find it prohibitively expensive to use as a sat nav. For that, check out a dedicated app like **CoPilot Live** (see overleaf).

Because CoPilot Live's maps are stored offline, you'll need a few GB of free space on your SD card. Wave goodbye to your MP3 collection.

CoPilot Live

If offline navigation is what you're after, CoPilot could be for you. It turns your phone into a fully operational voice-guided sat nav device. Features include detailed 2-D and 3-D maps, speed camera alerts, and live traffic and fuel price updates. Packages are available for different zones, starting at around $20 for the US, and $70 for Europe, with individual country maps available for around $30 a pop.

RMaps

RMaps allows you to search maps and track your route. It accesses maps online from a long list of switchable sources (Google included) and can cache these to your phone; scroll around an area you're due to visit and you can navigate it later offline.

MapDroyd

A basic map viewer offering free offline vector maps powered by **OpenStreetMap**. It can pinpoint your location via GPS but doesn't offer any search or navigation facilities. Still handy as a reliable backup map if you're travelling.

Compass

It's not like there's a shortage of compass apps out there, but we thought we'd try a few out so that you don't have to. This one from Snaptic has great-looking skins, can track your movements and upload them to their **3banana notes** service.

By tracking your movements and then uploading them to **Google Maps**, you can use My Tracks as a nifty way to create a detailed journey log.

My Tracks

My Tracks records your GPS location, tracking you and showing your time, speed, distance and elevation while hiking, cycling, running or just wandering around. You can visualize your tracks on **Google My Maps**, share them with friends, tweet them in **Twidroyd** and upload statistical data to Google Spreadsheets. If hiking's your thing, get the best **Compass** app too (see p.149).

internet
apps

Dolphin in action. Drag to the left for a sneaky toolbar, drag to the right for all your bookmarks, which can be dragged and rearranged. The tabs and address bar can be hidden by entering full-screen mode (available from the sidebar so you don't have to exit out to a settings page to get them back).

Dolphin Browser HD

Dolphin HD is a lightning fast, heavily featured web browser for Android™ 2.2 (if it doesn't work with your Android version you can still find the non-HD version in the Market). It looks and feels more like a desktop web browser than most, supporting add-ons (including the indispensable AdBlock), multi-touch pinch zoom, tabbed browsing, RSS feeds, bookmark sorting and sync with Google™ Bookmarks (something the stock browser doesn't even do) and full-screen mode. It also sports a password manager and assignable gesture commands. All this, and it's free.

Opera Mini's "speed dial" is an easy-access grid of bookmarks on your start page. Among other features, Opera supports tabbed browsing and full-screen mode.

Opera Mini

Opera Mini is the mobile version of the popular Opera desktop web browser. Like the other Android browsers, it manages to combine a rich feature set with a simple layout. Where Opera stands above the rest is in its powerful bookmark management, supporting folders – an important feature if you have more than a handful of bookmarks – and Opera Link, a feature that syncs bookmarks with the desktop Opera browser. Also useful is the ability to switch off images and make use of Opera's compression technology to speed up browsing and reduce mobile data costs.

Fennec for Android. This early pre-release is already sporting a lot of ingenious bells and whistles.

Fennec

Still very much a work in progress, Fennec is Mozilla's mobile version of the Firefox browser. We've been keeping an eye on its development and so far it's looking pretty fine. Features include scrollable sidebars, powerful add-on support, a Firefox-like Awesome Bar with one-touch bookmarking and tabbed browsing. It also supports Weave Sync, Mozilla's supercharged bookmark, tab and password syncing technology. You wouldn't use the pre-release version as your default browser, but for a sneak preview you can give it a try from the QR code above.

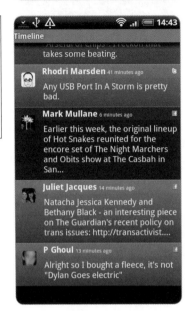

TMN Pond combines Facebook updates, blogs, newsfeeds and just about anything else. You may never need to open a web browser ever again.

TMN Pond

TMN Pond is a social network publisher and aggregator (see p.106) that'll bring your Facebook, Twitter, Flickr, LinkedIn, YouTube™ and other subscriptions together in one place. You can reply to posts, filter updates by site and post your own to individual or multiple sites.

You'll need to get an account with web.Pond.pt and set up your various sites and logins from there, but once done you won't have to worry about it again. You can also add other sources (RSS feeds, blogs and so on), and link to your own blogs and feeds so that you can publish to them, too.

It doesn't offer all the functions of the full site but the official Facebook app is snappy to use and has all the most useful bits. The scrollable gallery along the bottom takes you to recent video links posted by your friends.

Facebook for Android

There are a few alternative Facebook apps out there but the official one will handle most of your needs. You can access the news feed, search and view friends' profiles and photos, post comments, access your inbox and view notifications. It's still missing Chat and a few other features, but integrates well with your phone's sharing functions.

If you want to try some of the other Facebook apps out there, start with **Bloo**, **Babbler** and **Fbook**. Facebook Chat can be handled by a few third-party IM clients, including **eBuddy Messenger**, **GoChat** and **Meebo** (see p.158).

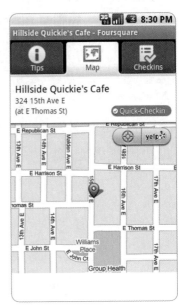

Foursquare is still in its infancy but could grow into a useful resource packed with information about venues around the world.

Foursquare

Foursquare is a location-based social networking service (or is it a game?) where you and your friends compete to "check in" to venues in and around your area and earn points. Once you've checked in to the same place more than anyone else you become the official Mayor (in Foursquare world, at least) of that venue, until someone else comes along and frequents the joint more than you. You can also create (and earn points for completing) personal to-do lists, and leave comments or tips about venues you've visited.

Meebo hooks up with all your other chat accounts so you'll be able to jabber away with everyone without hopping between apps.

Meebo IM

If you're an instant messaging addict, Meebo will handily consolidate all your accounts into one place. You can chat with people on Google Talk™, Yahoo!, AIM, Facebook, ICQ, MySpace, Jabber and MSN Chat, as well as Meebo itself. You can also provide status updates and view archived conversations.

Another popular messaging client worth a look is **eBuddy Messenger**, which has a similar feature set but can also run in the background and send notifications when someone wants to chat.

media and camera apps

DoubleTwist gives iTunes-esque integration between your computer and phone, making it easy to move your tracks around without rummaging through file browsers.

DoubleTwist

We've already mentioned DoubleTwist's desktop app (see p.108) and how it can, among other tricks, sync media with your phone. At the Android™ end of the equation there's this versatile media player. Standard features allow you to browse by artist, album, song or playlist, and you can rate songs, play video and grab podcasts. It'll also display album art a lot more readily than some other media players we've tried.

For media players that lack the sync capabilities, but sport extra features such as links to band info and scrolling song lyrics, check out **TuneWiki** or **Diggin**.

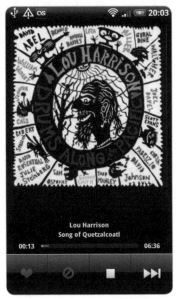

Last.fm – it's like having your own personal radio station. The two red buttons on the bottom left let you love or hate certain tracks, and the app will adjust its feed accordingly.

Last.fm

Pick an artist or genre and this app will build a playlist for you and stream it to your phone. Last.fm also "scrobbles" your music listening habits from your media player, uploading play counts to your page online and feeding you similar artists and recommendations. Tracks link up to an encyclopedia of information about each artist. Part-social network app, it also lets you view the details and stats of other users with similar tastes. If you're in the US, you can also check out the **Pandora**, **Grooveshark** and **MOG** apps, which offer services a bit like these.

If you regularly use your computer as a media centre for music and video, it's worth spending a minute or so to set up Gmote – before you know it you'll be skipping songs from the sofa.

Gmote

Gmote turns your phone into a (Wi-Fi/3G) remote control for your computer's media player. As well as installing the phone app, you'll need to download the small Gmote server program to your computer and create a password. From there you'll be able to browse and launch any media to play on the computer itself or streamed wirelessly to your phone.

There's also a function that transforms the phone's touchscreen into a wireless keyboard and mouse controller, as well as the ability to navigate and launch websites on the computer.

Did you work late and miss tonight's episode? You can watch it from your phone on the train home (assuming you've got mobile data to burn).

myPlayer

myPlayer accesses the BBC's iPlayer catchup TV and radio service and streams its contents to your phone, handy if you don't have the Flash-enabled browser required by the iPlayer website. Unfortunately for those outside the UK, this still doesn't let you access the service.

It can also stream live TV and radio (**Menu > View**) and streaming can be set to low quality for use over a 3G connection. Users running 2.2 and later can, however, use iPlayer directly by pointing their Flash-enabled web browser to bbc.co.uk/iplayer.

Qik brings point-and-click simplicity to live video streaming and makes sharing with Facebook, YouTube and the like a doddle.

Qik

Qik is a service that allows you to stream live video from your phone's camera over the web. Set yourself up with a free account at qik.com, install the app, and you'll be able to broadcast in real time to the world (or, if you prefer, just to the people you choose). The live videos are archived on the site so they can be played back later, too. Qik also supports live sharing to Facebook, Twitter and MySpace, as well as YouTube™ and Livestream.

A premium subscription ($4.99 per month) gives you video chat and video mail, among other features.

Simple but effective, Google Listen provides the podcast client that's missing from the box. And you can manage your Listen subscriptions from Google Reader™ on your computer, as well as from the Listen app itself.

Google Listen™

Like most Google™ products, the controls for Google Labs™ app for listening to podcasts and web audio are intuitive and easy to use. You can search for podcasts based on keyword and subscribe to your favourites (subscribed feeds are flagged as soon as new episodes become available), listen now or queue them up for later.

For a more sophisticated podcast and RSS reader, try **DoggCatcher**. It costs $6.99 but streams video as well as audio, gives recommendations based on your feed subscriptions and has a whole load of other useful features.

As well as searching and streaming a vast number of stations, Wunder Radio can locate local stations for you based on your GPS location, to feed you local weather and travel news.

Wunder Radio

Listen to thousands of global radio stations and other audio streams with this colourful little app. You can search among over four hundred sport, talk and music genres and sub-genres encompassing everything radio has to offer. Audio quality is limited by the output of the station you're listening to, but the streaming is consistent and smooth.

If you find a station you're into, you can save it to a favourites list for further listening. You can also add URLs of your own if you can't find what you're looking for. It's $6.99 but will provide you with all the radio you could ever need.

Flixster is a moviegoer's toolkit. Get instant access to a vast database of news and reviews, trailers and listings, all from this free app.

Movies by Flixster

Like the **IMDB** app for Android (also worth a look), Flixster is a movie buff's dream. You can check out new and forthcoming movie and DVD releases and view high-quality trailers. Then browse local cinema listings, locate cinemas on Google Maps™ and even find nearby restaurants.

The app also gives access to film reviews, from critics, other Flixster users and rottentomatoes.com. At present you can't submit your own reviews directly from the app, but you can rate films (via either your Facebook account or a Flixster account if you have one).

Cosmic tones. Ethereal Dialpad makes it easy to throw out blissful ear candy at its default settings. Tweak it a little and you can make things a bit more interesting.

Ethereal Dialpad

A deceptively versatile musical instrument for your phone. Move your finger around the touchpad to make delightful washy tones. The display can be switched between a number of pleasing skins, including a grid view, which gives you a better idea of what's going on. Hitting the preferences menu tab opens up an array of options for different scales and effects (including a spooky Theremin mode).

Other musical toys available for your phone include **Solo** (for the guitar hero in you), **Tub Thumper** (a drum machine) and **Sixteen Bars**, a mobile studio aimed at rap artists.

Vignette offers convincing photo effects for your phone's camera, applying professional-looking filters and borders to your shots.

Vignette

The stock Android camera app does its job admirably, but spend five minutes with Vignette and you'll be hooked. It comes with over sixty camera and film effects and twenty frames, including various film grains, a very convincing Polaroid simulation, toy camera and Technicolor. Suddenly anywhere you point your camera will give you breathtaking and stylish images. Vignette costs £2.99. A free demo version includes all of the features in the full version but will only takes low-res pictures. Or, for a snappy free (but less featured) alternative, try **FXcamera**.

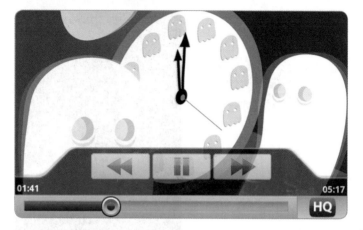

Flash opens up a wealth of online content. Streaming video and Flash-oriented websites and games can all be accessed from your phone's web browser. Pre-2.2 users should try the **Skyfire** web browser as this also offers streaming Flash video support.

Adobe Flash Player

If you're running Android 2.2 or later you can now use the web browser to access all kinds of streaming media content thanks to Adobe's Flash Player plugin. For a quick taste of what's on offer, point your browser to m.flash.com. Plus, of course, with Flash enabled, you can use YouTube™, Vimeo and any number of subscription-based streaming TV services like those offered by tvcatchup.com or clicker.com.

reader
apps

Droid Comic Viewer (aka ACV) renders images beautifully and makes the reading process easy with its intuitive zoom, fit to screen, scroll and auto-rotate functions.

Droid Comic Viewer

A simple, lightweight comic, manga and image viewer from the people at robotcomics.com. It'll open image files in most standard formats (.cbz, .acv, .cbr, .gif, .jpg, .png and .bmp) and can also read directly from compressed RAR and ZIP folders. It can read image folders with a long-press.

It's also worth taking a peek at **Vintage Comic Droid**, which allows free access to a vast library of vintage comics.

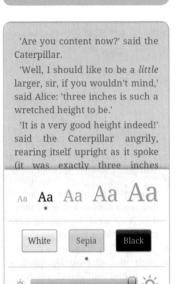

'Are you content now?' said the Caterpillar.

'Well, I should like to be a *little* larger, sir, if you wouldn't mind,' said Alice: 'three inches is such a wretched height to be.'

'It is a very good height indeed!' said the Caterpillar angrily, rearing itself upright as it spoke (it was exactly three inches

Aa **Aa** Aa Aa Aa

White Sepia Black

You'll need an account with Amazon before you can use your Kindle app, and you have to bounce out of the app and into your web browser to actually visit the Kindle store.

Kindle

Amazon's Kindle app syncs with your already purchased Kindle books and lets you read them through a pleasant but slightly limited interface. Navigating around is a doddle, with bookmarks and a location slider. Like most eBook readers it'll auto-save the last page you were reading. At the time of writing, you can't sync your bookmarks with other devices or search the text of your books.

Other book giants have their own readers, also worth a look – Barnes and Noble's **Nook** and Borders' **Kobo**.

Downloaded books appear on the shelves of a nice wood-effect bookshelf for your perusal. Pipe and slippers optional.

Aldiko

Aldiko is a beautifully crafted book reader that lets you download from thousands of free public domain and Creative Commons titles. It offers standard features like bookmarks and swipe navigation, but also some useful additions such as swiping up and down the left edge of the screen to adjust brightness, without having to enter the settings menu. If you tire of the thousands of literary classics on offer you can import your own (non-DRM) ePub books or add URLs to search other online book catalogues. For reading other eBook formats, check out the excellent **Laputa** and **FBReader**.

education
apps

Google Earth is a lot of fun to play around with but you may have to delete other apps to make room for it to install and run properly. Keep an eye on your battery levels too.

Google Earth™

Earth is like a supercharged Google Maps™. You can zoom in and out, browse different layers of geographical information, search for sites, businesses and cities, pinpoint your GPS location, and so on. Google Earth, however, takes all this a step further, with Wikipedia layers, stunning 3-D renditions, and a "look around" mode, which lets you rotate around the horizon from your chosen viewpoint. Once in look around mode you can toggle it off to move about the landscape at that elevation. Tapping the compass brings you back to satellite view.

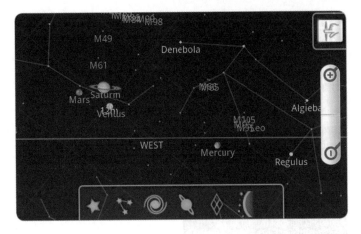

Google Sky Map uses your phone's GPS, compass and accelerometer to pan across the cosmos as you move your phone around. Can't find your home planet? Use the search function to point you in the right direction.

Google Sky Map™

Turns your phone into a window on the night sky. Simply point in the direction of a star or constellation to find its name. You can toggle layers to view stars, planets, grid lines, the horizon and "Messier objects". If you're looking for a particular celestial body, type its name and a pointer will guide you around till you find it. For more astronomical tomfoolery, check out **Celeste** and **Deluxe Moon**.

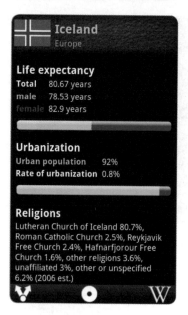

Iceland
Europe

Life expectancy
Total 80.67 years
male 78.53 years
female 82.9 years

Urbanization
Urban population 92%
Rate of urbanization 0.8%

Religions
Lutheran Church of Iceland 80.7%,
Roman Catholic Church 2.5%, Reykjavik
Free Church 2.4%, Hafnarfjorour Free
Church 1.6%, other religions 3.6%,
unaffiliated 3%, other or unspecified
6.2% (2006 est.)

From the population of Papua
New Guinea to the military
spending of Mexico, FactBook
has world facts covered.

FactBook

An informative reference app that provides a neat interface
for browsing collated information from the CIA World
Fact Book and United Nations data and statistics. You can
browse or search by region, country or rankings, compare
one country to another, and view detailed info and stats
on any country in the world. Turn your phone on its side
while reading about a country and your screen switches
to a slideshow of images fetched from Flickr. FactBook is
available for free, or for $2.99 without ads.

Want to test your newly acquired knowledge? Try **GeoQuiz**.

Memory Trainer's colourful puzzles help keep your brain ticking over. After a few rounds you can check on your progress over time to see if there's been any improvement.

Memory Trainer

Keep the cogs turning with this gentle mental workout. The app runs you through a series of simple tests, gradually increasing difficulty to task your working memory, "chunking" (your ability to break up information into more manageable chunks), spatial memory, focus and concentration skills. Exercises like these, performed daily, are meant to help improve the memory, and even reduce the risk of Alzheimer's disease. It certainly won't do you any harm. For more brain training, try **Math Workout** and **Ringz**.

Trippo Mondo's accuracy is about what you'd expect from an automated translator; it works best for short phrases.

Trippo Mondo

Trippo Mondo is a lightweight, reasonably powerful language translation tool. Type in a phrase and it'll bounce it back at you in any of the thirty supported languages. It'll also speak translations for you at an adjustable speed, with relatively accurate pronunciation. Pressing the little blue envelope button lets you share text translations via email, SMS, or any of your synced social network accounts.

For voice-to-voice (as well as text-based) translation, try **Google Translate™** or one of the individual **BabelFish Language Packs**, available for free from the Market.

The more you play, the more compelling it gets. Keep with it and you might accidentally learn something.

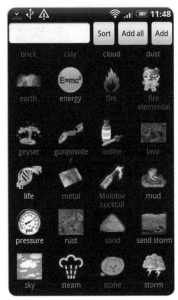

Alchemy

An addictive and (kind of) educational(ish) game that starts you off with the four basic elements of fire, water, earth and air. You drag these around to combine them with each other to make new elements, and then drag those around to combine into other elements. Eventually you'll begin to make more and more complex forms – life, algae, electricity, vampires – where will it end? Dragging any of these elements into the question mark icon reveals an encyclopedia entry for that item, replete with Wikipedia links to additional information. Educational after all, then.

Cheval's "Palais Idéal". The signs on the right read "Travail d'un seul homme" (Work of only one man) and "Défense de rien toucher" (Touch nothing).

2. Palais idéal

Cheval began the building in April 1879. He claimed that he had tripped on a stone and was inspired by its shape. He returned to the same spot the next day and started collecting stones.

Instant access to Wikipedia's millions of articles with a minimum of fuss, and it provides a handy search widget for your home screen, too.

Wapedia

One of many Wikipedia viewers out there, Wapedia is fast and well presented. What more could you ask for? Well, for starters, from the home page you can search or browse by category, what's in the news, popular content or random articles. The search bar auto-populates with suggestions as you type, so you'll rarely need to enter your full query. Articles are well formatted for mobile viewing, but if you don't like what you see it's fully tweakable. If you need to, you can switch from Wikipedia to a host of other wikis for reference, entertainment, humour, games, health and so on.

lifestyle
apps

You never have to stick your hand out of the window again. WeatherBug (Elite version pictured here) accesses the largest network of professional weather stations in the world.

WeatherBug

If you need a weather app, WeatherBug has all points covered – UV data, pollen count, temperature, lightning strikes, humidity, air pressure, wind speed, cloud cover – anything you could possibly need to know. You can peruse the forecasts for your saved locations from the app, or make use of the Google Maps™ integration, where long-pressing an area gets you an instant report.

WeatherBug is free from the Market; an ad-free "Elite" version ($1.99) offers live wallpapers, additional map layers, forecast and map widgets and live radar animation.

Video calls, as you'd expect, eat up a lot of battery power and data bandwidth, so unless you have Wi-Fi or unlimited data over 3G on tap, you may find this too resource-hungry to use when out and about.

Fring

An integrated messaging and VoIP service available on many platforms, Fring's Android™ incarnation offers free international video chat with other Fring and SIP users over Wi-Fi and 3G, which you can take advantage of if your phone has a front-facing camera. Skype is no longer supported.

If you just want a solid VoIP client without the extras, try taking **SIPDroid** or **Linphone** for a spin.

Qype, one of the many public review communities springing up across the Internet, helps remove the trial and error from your nights out.

Qype Radar

Looking for a place to eat? Qype feeds you other people's reviews of restaurants, bars, cafés, takeaways and venues in your area. You can do a quick search based on your location or use its slick interface to browse for particular venues by name or type. Qype's community of reviewers (of which you are now potentially a member) provides recommendations, star ratings and photos which you can peruse to get a better idea if a place is your cup of tea.

Similar services to try out include **Yelp** and **Google Places**™. For hassle-free restaurant reservations, try **OpenTable**.

Trip Journal's leathery, yellowed interface adds a scrapbook-like finishing touch to a well thought out and easy to use travel diary.

Trip Journal

A great way to share your travel experiences in real time with friends and family. Trip Journal tracks and maps your location while you upload photos, video and journal entries, and makes it all instantly available through your social network of choice. It integrates with major online services like YouTube™, Flickr, Twitter, Facebook and Google Maps and lets your friends view your progress and make envious comments.

Thinking of planning a trip? Check out **Kayak** for flight and hotel reservation management.

CardioTrainer helps you organize and plan your exercise schedules and track your fitness levels. It even calculates the calories you've just burned, based on your weight (which you have to enter, it doesn't turn your phone into a set of bathroom scales, silly).

CardioTrainer

CardioTrainer is a fitness and weight loss trainer that tracks your activity and keeps a record of your progress. It uses GPS and an accurate pedometer while you're running, walking, skiing or performing any other exercise (you can select the exercise type before the workout so that the results can be filtered later), and uploads the results to an anonymous account online which you can access later. You can get schedule reminders and set goals to achieve. It also supports some plugins from the Market, like **Racing**, which lets you challenge your own best times.

Cab4Me Lite

Simple app. Two tabs. First tab shows your location on Google Maps. Second tab shows a list of cab companies in your area. Press the button, call a cab. A future version promises push button booking without the phone call.

Car Locator

Car parks will never get the better of you again. Car Locator lets you save your location when you park up and then directs you back later on. You can send the location by phone or email to someone else too. This code links to the free trial. Full version costs $3.99 from the Market.

Pkt Auctions eBay

Easy to use app for eBay addicts, which includes live countdowns for auctions with less than a minute to run, a barcode scanner and a Price Check function that lets you view searched items finishing within your price range.

Never miss another show. Gigbox keeps you up to date with who's playing in your town, or indeed any other town on the planet.

Gigbox

For fans of live music, Gigbox hooks up with your Last.fm or Gigbox account to inform you when your favourite bands are playing in town. You can also search for gigs by location, venue or artist, add events to your calendar and find them on a map.

Once you're at the gig, the app enters Live mode, wherein you can chat with other audience members (as opposed to actually talking to them face to face, god forbid) and publish pictures and ratings to mygigbox.com from your phone.

You want more? Try **GigStar** and **Tunably**.

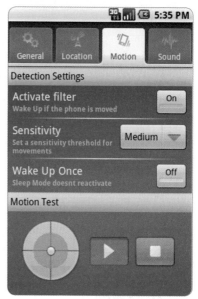

Burning the candle at both ends again? Sweet Dreams' inbuilt motion sensor will figure out that you're not in bed and keep your phone live till you're good and ready to settle down.

Sweet Dreams

Why turn it off when you can fine-tune how your phone behaves while you slumber? Turn notifications, ringers and alerts on and off to suit your needs. Beyond just setting it to switch modes at a certain time of night, you can adjust motion sensors, location and sound level filters so that the app can figure out if you're still up or not and act accordingly.

Ubertweakers can probably achieve all this with the **Tasker** app (see p.144), but Sweet Dreams hands you it all on a big soft pillow. For a stylish bedside clock incorporating similar features, check out **Bedside**.

Kidoikoiaki

Ever been in one of those situations where everyone brought something along for the trip and you had to work out how much money everyone owed everyone else? This app will quickly work that out for you. No more quibbling over shared expenses.

Google Shopper™

Kind of a reworking of other Google™ products in the name of buying stuff, Shopper lets you snap product barcodes and cover artwork for instant online price comparisons. For barcode-only snapping but with local shop results, check **ShopSavvy**.

Handcent SMS

Not happy with the texting facility your phone currently offers? Handcent's many features include popup notifications, unread message reminders, pre-composed quick replies, batch deleting and more. An alternative worth a look is the popular **ChompSMS**.

fun and
games

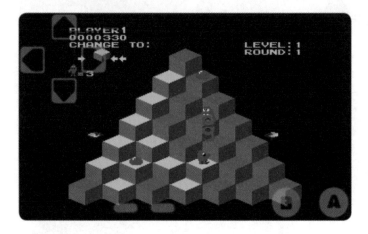

Retro gaming fun from NESoid. The simplicity of games like Q*bert (above) lend themselves well to a tiny touchscreen.

NESoid

One of the many classic console emulators available for Android™. This one plays vintage Nintendo games through a user-configurable touchscreen interface. To play games you'll need to download compatible game ROMs from sites like romnation.net or romfind.com to your SD card, anything with a .nes suffix should work. Other emulators are available – **Snesoid**, **GameBoid**, **Gearoid**, **Xpectroid** and more.

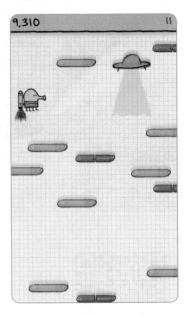

Doodle Jump's cute Doodler character resembles something you may have scribbled in the margins of your school math books.

Doodle Jump

This addictive iPhone hit has now been ported to the Android platform. It's an accelerometer-controlled platform game where you bounce a little green fella up the screen, earning points by zapping baddies with blobs of snot. Your route is littered with jetpacks, propeller hats and other power-ups to help you along the way. While Doodle Jump is something of a modern classic and the hand-drawn graphics and simple controls make it a lot of fun to play, at $3.49 you may find yourself drawn towards similar free games like the increasingly popular **Abduction!**.

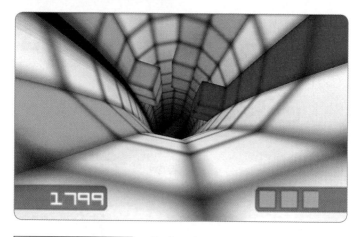

The best thing about this ride is that there's no swimming pool full of screaming kids at the other end of it. If you're the kind of person who reacts physically by ducking and diving when playing onscreen games, you probably shouldn't play this on a busy train.

Speedx 3D

Fast-paced accelerometer-controlled game that has you twisting your way down a hypnotic 3-D tunnel avoiding the obstacles as you go. Tilt the phone to spin clockwise or anticlockwise. The tunnels open out into flat plains and suddenly you're faced with the added challenge of not speeding off the edge. Speedx costs £0.99 from the Market.

For more 3-D racing action, check out **Speed Forge 3D**.

It looks simple enough but start tumbling this block around the austere maze and you'll find yourself hooked trying to navigate the limited surface area.

Amtalee

Nicely executed 3-D puzzle game where you have to shuffle the block towards the exit hole without falling off the edge of the maze. After a few easy levels to get you started, Amtalee offers increasingly difficult spatial conundrums to solve, with bridges that need to be switched on, teleports and collapsing tiles. The full game costs $3.99, but you can try out a free version with fewer levels using the QR Code above.

If you're a fan of letter games you won't be able to put this one down. Better call your friends and let them know they won't be seeing you for a while.

Lettered

A compelling and disorienting game that falls somewhere between Tetris and Scrabble. Tilt or rotate your phone and the letters slide around. Freeze letters in place and move the other letters around them to make words which you can then swipe away. New letters fall in from the top of the screen every few seconds. Can you clear enough words before the screen fills up? It also has a Boggle-like mode where you have to find as many words as you can from a random grid. A nice touch with both modes is that you can set the size of the grid. Another nice touch is that it's free from the Market.

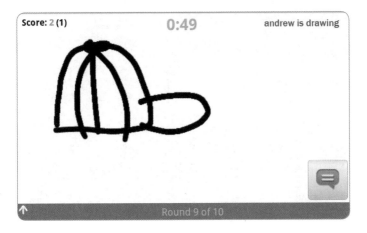

Score: 2 (1)   0:49   andrew is drawing

Round 9 of 10

Could it be a sieve? An igloo? A hat!
Maybe it's a hat! It's a delight just
watching other people's drawings
appear on the screen – a bit like
playing Pictionary with a ghost.

What the Doodle!?

A real-time online multiplayer drawing game. Join a match
and in a few seconds you'll be trying to guess the words your
opponents draw. When it's your turn, your word will hover
on the screen for a few seconds and then off you go. Points are
scored for guessing or having your picture guessed correctly
before the time limit is up. The full game costs £2.99, with a
perfectly usable easy-mode-only version available for free.

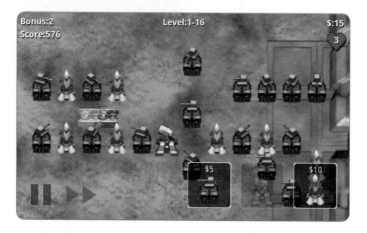

Why can't we all just get along? Robo Defense is set in a futuristic world where tanks cost five bucks, while magical slow-you-down-beam lava lamps are a snip at ten a pop.

Robo Defense

One of the better "Defense" games out there and a good introduction to the genre. The object is to gun down the bad guys as they try to run into your base. You place gun turrets at strategic points outside and hope you have enough firepower to keep them at bay. Killing the bad guys earns you money, which you can spend on more big guns to kill yet more bad guys. You can buy it for $2.99, or try the free trial.

custom
stuff

In its native form LauncherPro takes the look and feel of the HTC Sense interface and builds from there. If you're not enamoured with your existing home screen's options, this app will give you plenty to play with.

LauncherPro

"Launchers" are basically replacement home screens for your phone, and LauncherPro is one of the best. It's simple, fast, completely customizable and very user-friendly. Among its many features are smooth-scrolling screen transitions, a shortcut dock, pinch to preview all screens at once, numbered notification icons and elastic scrolling. LauncherPro is free, with a Plus version that includes widgets available for $2.99. For other options, check out **ADW.Launcher**, **Helix** and **Home++**. You can chop and change between all these home screens using the **Home Switcher** app.

Luna Surface - Alan Silva

MP3, 44100 Hz, 256 kbps, 1687.93 seconds

Start: 19.13
End: 21.43

Quick, simple sound editing without any messing around on your computer. Ringdroid lets you manipulate your music collection and assign clips as ringtones, alarms or notifications, or even record your own from scratch.

Ringdroid

Take complete control of all of your phone's ringtones and notification sounds. Ringdroid lets you pick any song or sound file currently stored on your phone's SD card and quickly crop it down to the part you want to use for your alert. The interface is intuitive – zoom in and out, swipe your way along the display, tap or press play to listen, and drag the start and end points to taste.

If you like the look of SlideScreen but you're not ready to commit to it as your default home screen, you can run it as a self-contained app without making the switch.

SlideScreen

A classy home screen replacement that draws info streams from your phone and any linked accounts. The top half gives you instant access to personal stuff like phone messages, emails, calendar and text messages, while the bottom half pulls together your public stuff – Facebook and Twitter feeds, stocks and shares, RSS feeds and so on. Long-press tap and swipe gestures trigger different options like removing a notification, opening the app or creating a new message. Slide the centre bar up or down to toggle the various feeds in more detail. Free, or $6.99 for the no-ads Pro version.

Open Home sports multiple home screens, live wallpapers and live folders, its own soft keyboard, and a snazzy rotating 3-D cube effect when you move from one screen to the next.

Open Home

Yet another launcher app to replace your phone's built-in interface with a custom one, Open Home is notable if only for the sheer number of skins, widgets and font packs available for it in the Android Market™. It includes some nice augmentations to your regular home screen, like a slide-out drawer where you can place apps and shortcuts so that they're accessible from anywhere, and the ability to rotate the home screen to landscape mode. It also lets you create shortcuts for custom functions. Open Home costs $3.99, with a free Lite version also available.

Power Strip lets you change settings, call up widgets and more without having to leave the app you're in and go back to the home screen.

Power Strip

Power Strip offers a handy dock for shortcuts, apps, folders and widgets. What makes it really nifty, though, is that you can assign it to your home button, making it accessible from anywhere, even within other apps. Useful if you want to toggle your GPS on when using maps, for instance, since there's no need to bounce back to the home screen and bring up the settings page. (You can still summon the regular home screen with a quick double-click of the home button.) For similar instant access to controls and apps, check out **SmartBar**.

productivity apps

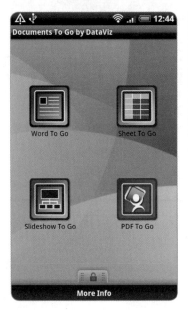

To get Documents To Go, download the free version (restricted to viewing Word and Excel files), from where you can unlock to the full version for $14.99. Also worth a look are Quickoffice Connect suite ($9.99) and OfficeSuite Pro ($14.99).

Documents To Go

Lets you view, edit and create Microsoft Word (.doc and .docx), Excel (.xls and .xlsx), PowerPoint (.ppt) and Adobe PDF files (its PDF viewer is one of the best available). Impressively sophisticated for its size, it offers features like word count, find on page, formatting tools, word wrap, multiple zoom levels and track changes, and support for password-protected files. There's also a Live Folder facility that lets you put a recently used files folder on your home screen. You wouldn't use it to write your memoirs but it's handy for last-minute editing while on the move.

With its clean, simple design, there isn't a whole lot to look at with K-9 Mail except your messages.

K-9 Mail

A highly regarded alternative to your phone's stock email and Gmail™ clients, K-9 is a stable, open-source email app that supports multiple accounts and standard mail server types (POP3, IMAP, Exchange, etc). It's stacked with features, including search, push mail, multi-folder synchronization, flagging and filing, signatures, configurable alerts, custom account colours, a global inbox and more. This is a great way to pull all your mail together in one program if you're not enamoured with the idea of running multiple accounts through Gmail.

One of the tricks up Voice's sleeve – text transcription of voicemail, which can be sent to you as SMS or email messages for you to quickly scan and then listen to or discard.

Google Voice

Google Voice™ provides you with one universal phone number and voice mailbox (currently available to US users only), giving you options to route all of your calls through the service, as well as forwarding calls to other numbers. It also allows you to make free national calls, and cheap international calls and text (SMS) messages.

As you'd expect, the app integrates fully with your contacts list. Although Voice is a free service from Google, your carrier may well impose additional charges, so double-check with them before you go crazy.

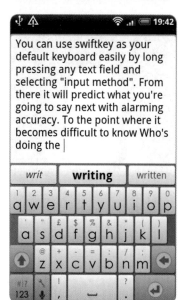

Have we known each other too long? SwiftKey scans your previous SMS messages to get an idea of what you type. After a while, it seems that all you have to do is repeatedly tap the space bar to approve the suggested words in order to get your sentence out.

SwiftKey

An alternative soft keyboard to the one that comes with your phone. It looks innocent enough, but SwiftKey has an impressive text prediction engine that seems to know what you're going to type next even before you do.

It doesn't just try and auto-complete as you type, it actually learns your writing habits and attempts to predict your next word, becoming increasingly accurate the more you use it. Simply hit the space bar to approve the suggested word, or tap one of the other suggestions either side. It also corrects spelling and grammar, and is free from the Market.

Edwin's simple, elegant interface. We just asked it "What are you actually useful for?" and got the unnerving reply, "I am a talking robot, here to serve you." Its speech recognition engine is excellent, and in our tests rarely got a word or phrase wrong.

Edwin

Speak your question and Edwin will speak the answer back at you. This is a clever speech-to-speech search engine that'll perform calculations and translations, give you weather reports, dictionary definitions and more. Once you're done asking it the time in Moscow, or how many inches in a light-year, you can give it commands to launch other apps, make calls, send tweets, toggle Wi-Fi on and off, and change other hardware settings. A fun way to mess around with your phone, Edwin could also be a useful accessibility tool for the vision impaired.

Google Gesture Search

Perform quick operations without having to browse through your phone's menus. Simply draw the first couple of letters of your required app or contact and a shortlist will appear. It can be set up so that you can trigger it with a simple flick of the wrist away from you and back.

Chrome To Phone

A plugin for Google Chrome™ and corresponding app for Android™ that lets you push the webpage you're viewing on your computer over to your phone's browser almost instantly. Firefox users can use this app with the **Send To Phone** add-on.

android2cloud

A simple app that lets you push web links from your phone to the Google Chrome browser on your computer. Works beautifully in tandem with Chrome To Phone (above) for painless switching between devices.

Bluetooth File Transfer

Allows you to use your phone to browse and manage files from any Bluetooth-ready device. It uses OBEX FTP or OPP to send and receive, and create, move or delete files and contacts. Makes light work of shuffling files between your computer and phone.

Inventory

Inventory lets you scan barcodes and enter details about an item. You can create categories and keep track of when you've lent it to someone. It'll even link lent or borrowed items with people from your contacts list.

Hertz

A simple and free sound recorder for uncompressed WAV files up to 44.1kHz (the equivalent of a CD). Useful for capturing sound or music when you don't want to compromise on quality. **Rehearsal Assistant**, **HiFiCorder** and **TapeMachine** are also worth a try.

Adobe Reader

From the PDF viewer options currently available for Android there's no completely satisfactory all-in-one app. Adobe's own reader is free, renders well most of the time, supports multi-touch gestures and has a useful reflow facility, but lacks bookmarking.

BeamReader

BeamReader costs $3.99 and supports bookmarks, text wrap view and text search. Rendering is acceptable, if occasionally a little slow. If you already have **Documents To Go** (see p.208), then you already have the extra functions offered here.

RepliGo Reader

Also $3.99, RepliGo integrates with Gmail and your web browser for previewing PDFs. It supports text search, bookmarks and hyperlinks, and has a single-column reading view. This and BeamReader have demo versions on the Market, so you can try out all three of the above for free.

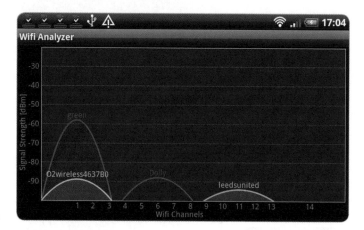

Dodgy connection? Get a quick window on who's battling you for the airwaves. Wi-Fi Analyzer presents its findings in a number of ways, focusing on either signal strength or channel usage. Keep a network cable handy if you're remotely configuring a Wi-Fi router, just in case something goes awry and you need to change your settings back.

Wi-Fi Analyzer

Shows all the nearby Wi-Fi access points and helps you improve your own Wi-Fi signal at home by finding a less crowded channel for your wireless router. If you're out and about, you can use it to find out which hotspot has the strongest signal and least traffic. With the free add-on Wi-Fi Connector, it even lets you switch connections from within the app.

With JuiceDefender battery level obsessives can tinker to their heart's content, setting different power-saving behaviours based on the time of the day, location, current battery level and more.

JuiceDefender

Squeeze every last bit of juice out of your battery with this automated power manager app. It lets you specify precise criteria for the behaviour of your phone's power-hungry Wi-Fi and mobile data functions. For example, you can set Wi-Fi so that it's only enabled when the screen is on, but schedule it to open up for a minute every so often to allow synchronization. The included widget lets you easily switch the app on or off and tells you how much juice you've saved. JuiceDefender is free, though you'll need the **UltimateJuice!** add-on (€2.79) to unlock some of its more esoteric features.

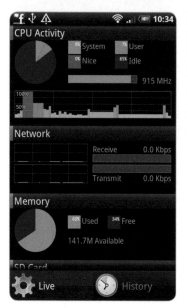

SystemPanel helps you figure out which apps are hogging your resources, giving you a much deeper level of information than Android's own application management screen. For a simpler task killer app, try **Advanced Task Killer**.

SystemPanel

SystemPanel combines a task manager, app manager and system monitor. It gives you a clear live view of which apps are using your phone's processor and memory, and monitors them over time to provide a detailed history of their activities. It'll also let you back up multiple different versions of apps (useful to fall back on if a free app you were using suddenly updates itself to a version that doesn't work with your phone). The full version costs $2.99, with a free Lite version providing the live view and task killer but no history monitoring or backup.

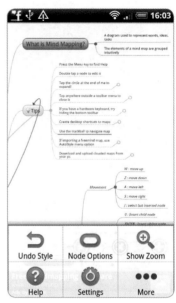

Navigate around your mind map by dragging around the touchpad, pinch-zooming and so on. Most of the app's core functions can be triggered via the touchscreen, with no need to jump through menus.

Thinking Space

This free mind-mapping tool lets you collect and organize your thoughts in a structured visual medium – a useful way to develop ideas and plans, problem-solve or brainstorm. You start by creating nodes, basically your core ideas, and then go on to create branches of sub-nodes and sub-sub-nodes. The relationships and connections can be easily rearranged and notes added. Once you're happy with your mind map, you can open it in Freemind (the free desktop version) or share it via Google™ Apps. Thinking Space is ad-supported, with an ad-free version available for £2.69.

With PhoneMyPC you can open up a program, make some changes, save them and email the new file to yourself – all from the other side of the world. Assuming, of course, that you remembered to leave your computer on…

PhoneMyPC

One of the many apps on the market that lets you control your computer from your phone over Wi-Fi or 3G. Install the app on your phone and the software on your PC, set up a password and you'll have a secure link between the two devices. You can operate your computer more or less as if you were sitting in front of it, using the phone's touchscreen as a virtual keyboard and mouse, or just take a quick snapshot to check the progress of a download. PhoneMyPC costs $9.99, but before you grab it, take a look too at **Remote Desktop Client**, **LogMeIn Ignition** and **PocketCloud**.

There are a few Pomodoro-type apps on the Market but this one's simple, very effective, and it's free. Tap the tomato to start or reset the timer, tap the sound and vibrate buttons to toggle how it lets you know your time is up. Right, now get to work.

Pomodoro Widget

What *is* that? A counting tomato? How exactly is a counting tomato going to make me more productive? In fact, Pomodoro uses a basic productivity technique: you set a timer for 25 minutes, during which you work on your given task, then take a break for 5 minutes, then work again for another 25. It's a great way to break up your workload into digestible chunks and set incremental deadlines. After four tomatoes (counted off in the bottom right), take a longer break, you've earned it. Looking for a straightforward timer? Check out **Ultimate Stopwatch** and **Timer**.

Build everything from simple games to educational quizzes to apps that tweet your GPS co-ordinates every time you say "carrots". Simply select the right blocks, combine them in the desired manner – and bosh, there's your app.

Google App Inventor

This web application (http://appinventor.googlelabs.com) lets you build your own apps from scratch without any programming knowledge (via your computer or phone's web browser). Instead of writing code, you build the app by combining blocks to specify what happens and when. There are blocks for pretty much every kind of function your phone is capable of, so with a little tenacity you can build any app you could conceivably want. Who knows? It could even end up in the next edition of this book.

security
apps

The KeePass database is encrypted with AES and Twofish, the most secure encryption algorithms currently known. So try not to forget your master password.

KeePassDroid

You probably have more accounts dotted around the Internet than you can keep track of. If you're wise, you'll have different passwords for all these accounts. KeePassDroid is a free, open-source password manager with a counterpart desktop PC app (available from keepass.info), allowing you to keep all your logins, passwords and PINs in one secure, encrypted database and access it with a single master password. The app will sync nicely with your computer if you keep the master file in Dropbox (see p.109) and access it from there. Also worth a peek: **1Password** (for Macs too) and **Password Keeper**.

A must-have for any competitive terror organization, drugs cartel or spy ring, the Pocket Enigma Machine is an evocative way to organize shady undertakings.

Pocket Enigma Machine

If text encryption is your kind of thing you might want to check out this German 1940s model. The Pocket Enigma Machine is a working simulation of the encryption devices used in World War II. Choose your three rotors, adjust their starting positions, tweak the alphabetical rings and patch letters together on the plugboard, then communicate these settings to the person receiving your message so that they can decrypt it at the other end. This recreation is lovingly rendered and even uses actual sound samples of the original device in action. The machine costs $2 from the Market.

App Protector Pro

App Protector Pro ($1.99) lets you password-protect applications on your phone, including inbuilt apps like SMS, Gmail, Photos & gallery and Calendar – anything, in fact, that you don't want other people getting access to for one reason or another.

Android Firewall

Automatically blocks unknown, unwanted or anonymous calls and text messages. You can set up multiple rules to block different callers or call types at certain times, hide selected numbers' calls and even prevent blocked calls going to voicemail. Costs $1.99.

Emergency Live Tracker

Another $1.99 app. This one will send email and SMS alerts showing your location to your pre-selected contacts in an emergency situation, say if you broke your ankle hiking or crashed your car in a remote ditch or got kidnapped or caught in an earthquake.

There are plenty of free solutions to back up your apps, but this one also backs up your contacts, call log, bookmarks, text messages, system settings, alarms, dictionary, playlists and more.

MyBackup Pro

Allows you to back up your phone to the SD card or to rerware.com's secure servers (up to 50MB). Backups can be triggered manually or scheduled to run automatically and you can select what you want to back up or restore (contacts, text messages, settings, etc) from a checklist. Useful if you're switching phones and want to move stuff across, or if you're in the habit of rooting your phone and want a quick way to restore your settings. It's easy to use and costs $4.99, though you can try it free for thirty days.

Lookout also provides a service where you can back up your contacts and photos to their remote servers, although if you already have your contacts synced via Gmail and routinely move photos onto your computer you won't need to use it.

Lookout

Lookout is a free suite of security tools including a virus scan, firewall and intrusion prevention. It's light on memory use so you shouldn't notice any impact on performance by having it running in the background. But perhaps its best feature is that you can use it to track down your phone if it gets lost or stolen, via an online mapping interface at MyLookout.com. From there you can also set your phone to draw further attention to itself by making a loud siren noise. For a total lockdown of a lost phone try **WaveSecure** (see p.143) or **Mobile Defense**.

Index

Index

Index